MURPHY HIMSELF

and Glenburnie

MURPHY HIMSELF

and Glenburnie

Gillian Newsum

with
Ian and Jenny Stark

The Kenilworth Press

Murphy Himself and Ian Stark powering over Henry's Corner, Badminton, 1991.

ACKNOWLEDGEMENTS

Many people have helped me with this book, but in particular I would like to thank Ginny Leng and Dot Willis for their valuable contribution to the information on Murphy's early years. I am also grateful to all those riders, trainers and officials who provided comments about Murphy, and, of course, to Ian and Jenny Stark for their time and patience in helping to produce the book.

PICTURE CREDITS

Barn Owl 28, 65 (both), 78, 79 (bottom), 80; *John Birt* 6, 58, 70 (top), 75, 83, 87, 88 (both), 91 (both), 94 (top row and bottom left), 95; *Eric Bryce* 34 (bottom); *Hugo Czerny* 11, 15, 23, 44, 51, 59; *Martin Dalby* 21, 43, 47, 69 (top), 70 (bottom); *Equestrian Services Thorney* 18; *Elizabeth Furth* 63; *Paul Green* 35; *Jan Gyllensten* 50; *Jack Higgins* 10; *Kit Houghton* 2, 16, 22, 26, 31, 33, 34 (top), 37, 38, 39, 40, 42, 54, 79 (top), end-papers; *Neil B. Jones* 94 (bottom right); *Bob Langrish* 24, 69 (bottom); *Peter Llewellyn (Photosport France)* 62, 74; *Trevor Meeks (courtesy Horse and Hound)* 8, 46, 72, 73, 82, 86, 90; *Gillian Newsum* 84; *Elaine Pickworth* 19; *Bob Thomas* 14.

Line drawings by C. Bromley Gardner, courtesy Badminton Horse Trials.

First published in 1992 by
The Kenilworth Press Ltd
Addington
Buckingham
MK18 2JR

© Gillian Newsum, 1992

British Library Cataloguing in Publication Data
A catalogue record for this book is available from
the British Library.

ISBN 1872082 327

Designed by Phil Kay
Typeset in Plantin by Textype Typesetters, Cambridge
Printed and bound by Bath Press, Glasgow

CONTENTS

"All our jumpers are natural winners!"

The Edinburgh Woollen Mill acquired Murphy Himself through a swap with Virginia Leng in the summer of 1988, and he was soon winning for Ian Stark, the rider sponsored by the company since the early days of his career.

The horse's sheer presence and athleticism have captured the imagination of the public and, like Desert Orchid, he has almost become public property. The company is thrilled to be the owner of such a magnificent animal.

WESTGATE
Westgate, the equestrian distributors, would like to thank Ian and Jenny Stark for all their support with Vetrap Bandaging Tape and Aerborn products.

FOREWORD

by Ian Stark, MBE

To have one superstar horse in a lifetime is the exception rather than the rule; to have two at one time is a very rare occurrence. 'The Boys', as Murphy Himself and Glenburnie are known, are two of these rare occurrences.

Murphy has always had a reputation for being quite a character, but until he came to Haughhead we didn't realise just how unusual a horse he is. From the day Murphy joined our yard we knew that he was rather special. He is a complete law unto himself.

In the winter when he runs out in the field with a crowd of other horses, even the youngest horse can bully him. By contrast, in the event season, when he is really fit and competing, nobody argues with him – not even me!

'Himself' does not really like to be disciplined or controlled and frequently makes his own decisions about life. I shall always remember the time when he bounced the Road Crossing in Stockholm. It felt so easy because he has so much scope, but watching it again and again on video, I know that I shall never have another horse like him.

Like most brilliant horses Murphy could probably have turned his talents to pure dressage or show jumping just as easily as to eventing; and Glenburnie would surely have been a top racehorse, for no other can accelerate with such speed and stamina at the end of a gruelling three-day event.

Murphy and Glenburnie are multi-talented individuals, second to none to ride, and I'm glad their stories are now being told. They are real 'stars' who deserve no less.

Ian Stark

Murphy Himself (left) and Glenburnie.

CHAPTER ONE

A Dubious Start

Murphy Himself was born in County Down, Northern Ireland, in 1979. He was a precocious foal who grew up fast and who has spent most of his life convincing people that he is a year older than he really is. Jack Higgins, his breeder, confirms that Murphy was born in 1979, a year after the official date of foaling stated on his registration papers at the British Horse Society Horse Trials Office, and on his passport. Given this information, it is hardly surprising that, following Ginny Leng's purchase of the young Murphy in 1982 (supposedly as a four-year-old), he continued to grow! Moreover, it means that Murphy competed in, and won, his first three-day event (in Avenches, Switzerland) at the grand age of five.

Murphy's parentage offered few pointers to the grey's future; to his abundant talent and sometimes wayward nature. When Ginny bought him she was told that he was probably by the Thoroughbred stallion, Royal Renown, but beyond that she knew nothing about his breeding. Murphy's mother was actually a half-bred chestnut mare by Cappagh Boy. She probably had a little Irish Draught blood in her from her dam's side, and she was only 15.3hh. Although broken as a three-year-old, Molly, as she was known, was put in foal as a youngster and never did any work. She had nine foals altogether, six of them by Royal Renown.

The distinctive grey colour of Murphy Himself comes from his father. Royal Renown, born in 1971, was a grey stallion by Gustav out of My Sweetheart (by Hard Ridden, a Derby winner). However, Royal Renown was not a successful racehorse. He was placed once as a two-year-old in Ireland; did no good as a three-year-old, and although he stood at stud in Ireland, only five of his progeny are registered with Weatherbys.

From this undistinguished background has emerged one of the greatest stars in eventing. Clearly, much of Murphy's success has been a direct result of his exceptional ability, but there is no doubt that if his life had followed a different course and he had not been lucky enough to have come into the hands of two of the best event riders in the world, he could easily have fallen victim to his own impetuous and often difficult temperament. Ian Stark, who has learnt to cope with Murphy's character by letting him, to a certain

Facing page: *Murphy competing with Ian at Belton Park, Lincolnshire, April 1992.*

Murphy as a foal in County Down, Northern Ireland. He was born in 1979.

extent, take the law into his own hands, is the first to admit that without the thorough and patient training that Murphy received from Ginny Leng, the horse could have become a liability – 'a shooting case'.

When Murphy was six months old Jack Higgins sold him to William Smith, who subsequently sold him on as a three-year-old to Ann Verdon-Jones. She saw Murphy at a sale while on a visit to Ireland. 'I was told he was by Royal Renown, but as he had no papers it wasn't possible to verify this, so I had to take him on trust. He was a more compact horse then, only 16.1hh, but he obviously hadn't finished growing. He was quite a wild-looking thing, with a long mane and tail, and he'd hardly been handled at that stage.'

At Ann Verdon-Jones' yard at Alfold, on the Surrey/Sussex border, Murphy happily took to lungeing and long-reining, but when it came to putting a rider on his back his attitude suddenly changed. 'He was very naughty. Very, very naughty,' explains Ann Verdon-Jones. 'There were four of us at the yard and he had us all on the floor in turn, at least three times each. When the lad who was working for me injured himself falling from Murphy, I decided that was enough. I was fed up with him, so I filled a couple of old, long leather riding boots with sand and strapped them either side of the saddle so they couldn't fall off (it's an old trick of mine, and it never fails).

'Then we let Murphy go in the school, and he went berserk. The more he bucked and leapt about, the more the boots slapped at his sides, but he couldn't get rid of them. Eventually he jumped out of the school, hitting the top rail of the fence and falling heavily on the landing side. He lay so still after the fall that I thought he was dead, but when I got up to him he just opened one eye and looked at me as if to say, "All right, you win."

'We never had a moment's trouble with him after that. He went like a hero. Within half an hour of backing him he was being ridden around the school in complete balance, and could even canter happily. He was always a lovely moving horse with tremendous presence, and I'm glad he learnt to cooperate by hurting himself and not from one of us having to have a go at him. I think if we'd done that he would have always mistrusted humans.'

When Murphy was advertised in *Horse and Hound*, Heather Holgate (Ginny Leng's mother) spotted the advertisement and Ginny went to see him. It was at the end of 1982, the year that Ginny had won a team gold medal on Priceless in the World Championships in Luhmühlen, but following the parade of medallists at Olympia, Priceless had become critically ill.

When Ginny first saw Murphy she liked his head, 'but it was seeing him trot that really excited me,' she said.

'It was while Priceless was ill,' wrote Ginny in her autobiography, 'that I bought a horse on my own, without either my mother or Dot [Willis] present, for the first time in my life. I was feeling very low because of P's condition and not at all in the right frame of mind for the cocktail party in Sussex which my sponsors [British National Life] had asked me to attend. The horse was advertised in *Horse and Hound* as a four-year-old strawberry roan, and since I would be passing the owner's place on the way to the party, I decided that I might as well take a look.

'I liked Murphy Himself's dark grey head (in fact he was mostly grey, with some bay hairs), but it was seeing him trot that really excited me because he had such wonderful movement. Doing my best to retain a non-committal expression, I watched while he was ridden towards some cross poles. He ran out at them three times. This horse is quite a character, I thought.'

Ginny rode him and decided to buy him on the spot – subject to a vet's examination. The price was £2,500. When she reached Mike and Angie Rutherford's house in Sussex, where she was staying overnight, she rang her mother, Heather to say she wanted Murphy to be vetted. Heather was dumfounded. She had suggested to Ginny that she go and look at the horse on her way to Sussex, but she had not meant her to buy him. Dot's response to the news was, 'Well, he must be special.'

CHAPTER TWO

Murphy with Ginny

When Murphy arrived at Ivyleaze it was generally agreed that he was indeed something special. Dot Willis, who has helped train Ginny for over ten years, explains: 'He is not the best-looking horse, but once you've seen him move that's it. Mind you, I've been told I'm a sucker for a good mover! The one thing that worried me was that he was quite big; he measured 16.2hh, but he looked bigger. But then those partnerships – a big horse and a relatively small rider – can work, and if they do they can be brilliant.'

Before this particular combination could be brilliant, however, there was a lot of work to be done, and Murphy was not a good pupil. Ginny found that she could never use a stick on him, otherwise he would rear and plunge.

Whenever she tried to teach him a new movement he would argue immediately without even waiting for her to explain what she was trying to do. As a matter of principle he would always fight first. 'You could not ask Murphy to do anything: you could only make suggestions,' says Ginny. 'We never got cross with him. We just kept repeating the question, and to start with he would rear and plunge – and when he did that you knew all about it – but we would keep going, not making a big deal out of it, and gradually he would accept what we were doing.'

Ginny's seemingly endless patience was tried again and again, but she was not going to be beaten by this horse. His brilliance was obvious; it just had to be channelled in the right direction. 'I think the only reason he decided to go for me was because I never got at him,' says Ginny. 'That doesn't mean to say we didn't discipline him, but we did it mostly by using the voice.

'When Murphy was a young horse he hated having anyone on his back. If you leant forward to pat him on the neck he would rear and kick back with his ears flat back. The same thing happened when you went over a fence; if you leant forward up his neck he would put his ears back and kick back at you. I used to lean over when he was standing still and give him Polos, and he gradually began to accept that that was all I was doing, but he still didn't really like it. He was a different character if you were standing on the ground, and he would be very affectionate, but he hated anyone

being on top. I think it was because he liked to feel that he was in charge, and he regarded the rider as a threat.'

Murphy has always had a mind of his own and if he decided he didn't want to do something he could be very awkward. At the first dressage test he ever did with Ginny they did not get very far because when Murphy halted at X he reared up and refused to move in any direction. Jumping could be just as difficult. Although he could jump brilliantly, he was never very enthusiastic about it at home, and, as a youngster, used to run out whenever possible. At his second novice event (at Windsor Forest Stud) Murphy got it into his head that he definitely did not want to go the way Ginny was planning to go, he wanted to go in another direction. He ran straight past two fences in the middle of the field, and although Ginny had both hands on one rein in an attempt to turn him it made no difference at all. Eventually she managed to stop him, but she then had to dismount and sort out his bridle because the bit had been pulled completely through his mouth.

After that unnerving episode Murphy settled down well, and he went through novice and intermediate events without any further mishaps. The first three-day event he did was at Avenches, in Switzerland, when he was, supposedly, six. (The doubts about Murphy's correct age crept in the following year when, at the age of seven, he seemed to have a set of six-year-old teeth.)

Murphy at his first three-day event, at Avenches, Switzerland, in 1984. Unbeknown to Ginny, Murphy was only five years old at the time, but he 'went like a dream' and won the event.

Facing page: *Murphy and Ginny going through the Lake at Badminton in 1988.*

Avenches was a great success. Murphy went 'like a dream' and won the event, after which Ginny returned to prepare her two top horses, Priceless and Night Cap, for the Los Angeles Olympics.

The following year, 1985, Murphy was prepared for the new three-day event at Chatsworth, which took place a month after Ginny had won the European Championships at Burghley. The event started well with Murphy and Mark Phillips' Distinctive being joint leaders after the dressage, but then Murphy ran into difficulty on the cross-country. It happened at the Dog Kennels, where there were three sets of rails involving two bounces. Murphy jumped in so boldly that he found himself uncomfortably close to the second element and impossibly close to the third. He somehow managed to get over the final rails and stay on his feet, but he jumped Ginny off in the process.

Finding himself on his own, Murphy decided to gallop back down the hill towards the steeplechase course. 'I still shiver when I think of the numerous ropes he jumped as he went flying off looking for action,' wrote Ginny. Luckily, as he paused for a quick nibble at the grass, someone managed to catch him (a difficult feat with Murphy at the best of times), so Ginny remounted and finished the course. Murphy jumped the remaining fences beautifully and, despite the fall, which was caused only by inexperience on his part, Ginny was delighted with him. 'What a star, I thought. Now he's proved he's got what it takes.'

> Elaine Pickworth – groom to Ginny Leng
> *Murphy's wicked sense of humour was never more apparent then when you wanted to catch him in the field. He would saunter over to you, all sweetness and light, devour the nuts you had brought to tempt him, then wheel round and trot off, kicking his heels. Sometimes he would circle you in trot, just out of reach. I often thought he just wanted to test out my boredom threshold.*

The following weekend Ginny took Murphy to Castle Ashby, hoping to finish the season on a better note. She decided to try changing his bit from his normal gag to the milder Dr Bristol, a move that she regretted as soon as she set out on the cross-country. Murphy took off at breakneck speed and continued in that vein for the rest of the course. Although he cleared all the fences it was not a happy experience for his jockey. Fortunately Ginny was able to ride him soon afterwards in some show-jumping competitions at the Markfield Equestrian Centre in Leicestershire, where he won both the Newcomers and the Foxhunter, so he did at least end the

Facing page: *At the Ice Pond Table at Chatsworth in 1985. Murphy had jumped Ginny off after a mistake at the Dog Kennels, four fences earlier, but he completed the course without further mishap.*

Jumping well out over Centaur's Leap at Burghley in 1986. It was Murphy's first major international event, and he led the competition from beginning to end.

season well – so did Ginny, for the year ended with her marriage to Hamish Leng.

The following June Ginny rode Murphy at the two-star three-day event in Le Touquet, France, where they led from start to finish; and in September that year they went on to win at Burghley, Murphy's first three-star international event. In three years Murphy had won three three-day events.

His victory at Burghley was one of the highlights of Ginny's career – despite the fact that she was already European Champion and had just become the new World Champion. To take a first-timer to Burghley and win was an outstanding achievement, and to Ginny the challenge of tackling the Burghley cross-country course on a young horse was comparable to the excitement of winning the World Championships in Gawler earlier that year. Furthermore, Murphy's immaculate performance there gave Ginny her fourth consecutive win at Burghley – a record unlikely to be surpassed.

As a tribute to Ginny's patience and training Murphy had bounded round the course at Burghley like an old-timer. He went into the lead after the dressage and stayed there, adding no more penalties to his dressage score. He proved to be very honest (at the Maltings Rails he was not on quite the right stride but still jumped successfully through the quick route), bold (he leapt into the Upper Trout Hatchery without a moment's hesitation) and deadly accurate (Ginny took the direct line at nearly every fence). The only obstacle where Ginny opted for the longer route was at the Zig-Zag, the fourth from home, because by then she was beginning to lose control.

Murphy's strength was the one slightly disturbing factor about his Burghley round, though it was only towards the end of the course that he started to 'take control'. As he had begun to tire he was leaning on Ginny. 'I never felt he was going to run away with me,' she explains, 'but he would not slow down because he was leaning on the bit and I couldn't have got him back to jump a trappy fence.'

Ginny was not unduly concerned about the problem which, anyway, was momentarily forgotten in the excitement of winning Burghley on this exceptionally talented young horse. However, it returned with a vengeance at the start of the 1988 season when

Handsome is as handsome does! Murphy at Ivyleaze after his winter holiday.

Murphy actually ran away with her. He had been prepared for Badminton the previous year, but when it was cancelled he had had most of the season off because Ginny was busy preparing for the European Championships with Night Cap, who was still her number-one horse. Murphy's first one-day event at the beginning of the following year was Kings Somborne. Perhaps it was because he was so delighted to be out eventing again, or because he was feeling stronger and fitter than ever; whatever the reason, Murphy decided he was going to have some fun. As he landed over the Trakehner at the top of the big hill there, he took off. 'He really meant it,' says Ginny. 'He tore off down the hill and I had to do a huge circle to pull him up.'

Heather and Dot had been standing at the bottom of the hill and were horrified by what they saw. The realisation that Murphy was becoming perhaps dangerously strong began to concern them both.

Ginny had known all along that Murphy was not going to be the easiest of horses to hold together because of his long back, but she had worked hard on the problem. She spent the best part of two years teaching him to shorten, to be more collected and engaged, as she feels very strongly that a horse will suffer less stress on the cross-country if he is properly balanced. 'I like my horses to go in a good rhythm, and to go safely,' explains Ginny. 'All the horses I have ridden have gone in the same way because that is how I have trained them.'

Murphy was no exception. 'He always wanted to leave out strides if he could, because he thought that was easier. But I knew that if he did he would get into trouble later on in his career, so I worked very hard on getting him to shorten and put in the correct striding. I was never frightened of the power. He was like a dream-machine to ride, but I did find it physically very difficult to get him to shorten coming into combinations because he was so long in the back.'

Although he had good paces, he was by no means the easiest of horses to train. The main problem was that he used to get bored at home, especially doing flatwork and show jumping. 'I used to have to work very hard on him, kicking all the way, so he wasn't really an enjoyable ride at home except when we were cantering. His attitude was that circles and shoulder-ins were very boring, and as he could do them already why should he bother to do them now?'

Facing page: *Ginny and Murphy at Stowell Park in 1987 in preparation for Badminton, which had to be cancelled that year because of torrential rain.*

Murphy jumping well in the Citation bit at Brigstock in 1988, three weeks before Badminton.

If Ginny got after him with a whip at home to wake him up she did not achieve anything. 'He would rear and plunge, and then go straight back to being dull,' she says. 'You didn't get any more engagement or roundness, you just got more of what you didn't want. So at the end of the day he won anyway, because you ended up being prepared to accept less than you really wanted.'

Ginny had to psych herself up each morning to ride him, planning what she would do to prevent him becoming bored. He was both mentally and physically draining, and as he became fitter and more mature, and his confidence increased, Dot sensed that Ginny's relationship with him was becoming more of a battle and less of a partnership.

Following the trouble at Kings Somborne Ginny tried some new bits and eventually settled on the Citation, a bit recommended to her by event rider Lizzie Purbrick. It worked well at Brockenhurst, Murphy's last outing before Badminton, so Ginny went to Badminton feeling reasonably confident that she had solved the problem. Since Night Cap had retired after the European Championships in Luhmühlen the previous year, Murphy had become Ginny's number-one horse. Although he had done everything in the book to qualify as her Olympic mount for Seoul, this was to be his first trip round Badminton. Ginny's other ride at Badminton that year, Master Craftsman, was even less experienced than Murphy.

Riding two horses at Badminton is hard work at the best of times, and to take two first-timers is a daunting prospect. However, everything started well when Crafty produced a good, relaxed test, which left him in fifth place after the dressage. Murphy's performance was not quite so straightforward. While working in the collecting ring he had been unnerved to see one of the Whitbread

Murphy on his best behaviour at Badminton in 1988. He did not manage to contain his excitement, however, and at the end of his dressage test he performed his own version of a levade as he came up the centre line.

drays rumbling past rather too close for comfort. Much to Ginny's relief, however, he did not react as violently as she had feared, but by the time he had reached the end of his dressage test he was ready to give his own little display – Murphy's version of a levade – which nearly landed them both in the judges' laps. 'I could have slaughtered him,' said Ginny. Murphy was placed fourteenth at the end of the dressage.

There were two obstacles on the cross-country course that particularly concerned Ginny. One was the Ski Jump and the other

Jumping boldly into the Lake at Badminton, 1988. Everything was going well at this stage.

the Coffin. Her worry at the Ski Jump was that Crafty would not pick up his front feet over the rail at the bottom of the hill. At the Coffin she was anxious that, because the rails were placed only a short distance from either side of the ditch, Murphy might try to bounce through this combination. Despite all his training he still had a tendency to do his own thing now and then.

Crafty was Ginny's first ride on the cross-country and, although he was quite strong, he went exceptionally well for her. The Holgate team were thrilled. In Crafty, Ginny now had an Olympic horse. In fact, as Dot points out, there was no real need for her to ride Murphy. 'We were ecstatic about Crafty, and still a little unsure of Murphy. I think we just didn't want her to go and overdo it.' But Ginny was not to be put off. 'I could sense a sort of a dread from Mummy, from Dot, and from everyone who was there with us. None of them, basically, wanted me to ride Murphy, though no one would say it. But I thought, "Well, damn it. I'm going..." '

Murphy's steeplechase round made everyone feel more at ease. It was controlled and sensible, and the Citation bit seemed to be working, so confidence was restored. The cross-country also started well, the only disturbing factors being that Murphy took a stride out both in front of the Pardubice Taxis and across the Centre Walk.

However, Murphy settled again after that. He jumped the next twelve fences, including the Lake and the Normandy Bank, beautifully. Then came the Ski Jump. All seemed to be going well, Murphy approached at a sensible pace, but the next thing Ginny knew was that she was being catapulted out of the saddle as Murphy launched himself out into space over the log pile at the top of the steep bank, and then galloped off into the distance.

'I think he did it because I was holding on to him and he jumped away from the bit. If I had given him his head just before he took off he would probably have seen the fence better and not have made that mistake. It was the first time on the course that I had asked him to trot and he seemed to say, "Why are we trotting? Let's go now." It may have been his way of telling me that he didn't like the amount of control I had him under, but I honestly think he just didn't assess the fence correctly.'

Ginny had landed with an ominous thud and was taken away in an ambulance. X-rays taken the following week revealed a dislocated ankle and bad bruising, but no broken bones, a diagnosis that

Ginny nursing her broken ankle at the bottom of the Ski Jump while Murphy gallops off . . . to Scotland. It was this fall at Badminton that changed the course of Murphy's future.

Ginny found difficult to accept (and which much later was found to be incorrect). 'I couldn't believe it when they said it wasn't broken. Certainly I don't wish ever again to be in the pain I endured on show-jumping day.' Determination to complete Badminton with Crafty and thus qualify him for the Seoul Olympics was uppermost in Ginny's mind as she steeled herself for the show jumping.

Remarkably, under the circumstances, Crafty jumped clear to finish in third place (behind Ian Stark, who was first and second with Sir Wattie and Glenburnie), and Ginny was able to enjoy a successful conclusion to Badminton. However, lurking in the back of her mind was the big question mark over Murphy's future. She knew that her mother and Dot had been concerned about Murphy's increasing strength, and his mistake at Badminton was likely to tip the balance of favour against him. She was right. The knives were out for Murphy.

Both Heather and Dot worked hard to convince Ginny that she should not continue to ride him. 'Dot and I very seldom put any pressure on Ginny,' says Heather, 'but I think after Badminton we did put quite a lot of pressure on her to get rid of Murphy. He worried me. When you have a fall from a horse like Murphy it is bound to be nasty because there is so much power behind it.

'This is a dangerous sport anyway, even when everything is going as well as possible. Murphy wasn't doing Ginny's riding any good, as he was pulling her forward constantly; and given time I think she probably would have lost her nerve, because you can't go on under those conditions and ride well.'

Indeed such was Heather's concern that she threatened never again to watch her daughter compete on Murphy. 'That really put me on the spot,' says Ginny. 'The whole point of my competing was that we should be able to enjoy it together.'

Dot sided with Heather. She sensed that Ginny's control of Murphy was borderline, and had been for some time, and although the Badminton incident wasn't the result of a serious lack of control it nonetheless indicated that the partnership was not truly moulded together. Murphy was taking too much out of Ginny, both physically and mentally, and there were other horses that needed her attention.

Ginny has always respected the views of her mother and Dot, and under pressure from them both her defences crumbled, but she never really accepted the decision to part with Murphy. For one thing, it was not good for her pride – she had never been beaten by a horse and she did not intend to be beaten by Murphy. At Badminton she felt that she had almost got things right with him. Then there was her personal attachment to him, made stronger by the fact that it had been her decision, and hers alone, to buy him, and because she had spent more time and patience on his training than on any other horse. She also appreciated that he was the most naturally talented jumper she had ever ridden, he was very intelligent and he had exceptional paces; in short, he was a brilliant horse. Giving all that up was not going to be easy. 'We argued a lot,' says Ginny, 'and although I eventually gave in I was never happy about the decision.'

Even when the decision had been taken it was not immediately clear how to proceed. The Holgates had received a fantastic offer for the horse from abroad, but Ginny, who had been a regular member of the British team for the previous eight years, was determined that Murphy should go to a British rider. It was also quite clear that he needed to be ridden by a man.

Ian Stark became the obvious choice. He, too, had been a regular team member since the Los Angeles Olympics; he had recently come first and second at Badminton, but of the two horses he rode there Sir Wattie was drawing near the end of his competitive career and Glenburnie was turning out to be very accident prone. Ian was in need of another top horse and he was one of the few riders capable of taking on a 'powerhouse' like Murphy.

CHAPTER THREE

A New Partnership

Unlike Ginny, Ian came from a non-horsey background. He had his first riding lessons at the age of ten, and it was not until 1982, when he was twenty-eight, that he gave up his job at the local DHSS office in Galashiels to concentrate on eventing. By that time Ginny, who is a year younger than Ian, had already represented Britain on two Junior teams (winning the individual and team European Championship gold medals in 1973) and on a winning senior team (1981 European Championships). Ian first rode for the British team at the 1984 Olympics in Los Angeles, since when he and Ginny have been firm friends.

Ian combines a natural talent with a strong competitive spirit. He is the sort of person who likes to operate at top speed, and there is a 'things must be done yesterday' feeling about his approach to life. As a youngster he could never be bothered with dressage: it was the excitement of galloping and jumping that drew him into the sport. Even now his patience for dressage is limited, whereas there is little to beat the thrill of cross-country riding (though driving cars at breakneck speeds and hurtling down ski slopes come a close a second). His riding style is influenced by his courage, his determination and sometimes his sheer audacity. Rarely does a cross-country round of Ian's fail to thrill spectators and to produce some drama or other. In contrast, Ginny's cross-country performances are renowned for their immaculate style and perfect control, a reflection of the endless patience put into the training of her horses. Could Murphy make the switch between two such different competitors?

The idea of selling Murphy had never really been a serious consideration for Ginny because, even with the money gained from such a sale, it would be almost impossible to buy a replacement at the right level. As it happened, though, Ian had a 16hh eventer called Griffin whom he had once offered, half jokingly, to swap with Master Craftsman. 'It was while we were travelling out to the event at Lion d'Angers, in France,' explains Ian. 'I was riding a horse called Yair, and Ginny had Master Craftsman. She didn't like him much at the time, because she thought he was too big and rangey, but Heather had persuaded her to persevere with him. On

Facing page: *Taking the fast route at the Folly at Gatcombe, 1991. Murphy is usually very accurate and holds his line well at obstacles like this.*

the journey we joked about swapping horses, but as Crafty went quite well in Lion d'Angers nothing more was said about it.'

After Ginny damaged her ankle in the fall from Murphy at Badminton she asked Ian to ride one of her young horses, Bally-hack, at Tidworth. The two got on quite well, so Ian took Ballyhack to compete at Breda, in Holland, and Ginny, hobbling about on crutches, went out to watch. It was there that discussions, at first light-hearted, started about a possible swap between Griffin and Murphy. As Griffin was only 16hh he was a little small for Ian, who had actually bought the horse for his wife, Jenny, but then pinched him back for himself when he realised the little gelding was quite talented! Now he was being offered a direct exchange between the slightly less experienced Griffin and a horse that was generally regarded as being one of the most brilliant eventers in the country.

Soon after returning from Breda Ian went down to Ginny's home at Ivyleaze, near Badminton, to see Murphy. As he was led out of his stable by Ginny's head groom, Elaine Pickworth, Ian's first response was: 'Goodness, he's ugly, isn't he?' He was no more impressed when he rode the horse. 'I took him in the outdoor arena and he just plugged round. I asked for a pair of spurs, then a dressage whip, but neither seemed to make much difference. Then I jumped a few fences on him, which he jumped all right but without much enthusiasm. Dot tried to reassure me that he wasn't like that at competitions, but I certainly wasn't very inspired. I couldn't understand why this horse, who looked so exciting and powerful when he was ridden by Ginny, didn't give me the feel of what I had seen.'

Ian returned home to Scotland, somewhat disillusioned. Jenny was delighted. She had been unhappy about the prospect of losing Griffin – her horse, after all – and she also felt they had quite enough horses to deal with at Haughhead without taking Murphy. 'I just thought, "Oh good, we won't have him then. Let's not take the matter further." '

However, Ginny, who had not been around when Ian tried Murphy, telephoned to explain that Murphy could be a bit lazy and bored at home, and that it would better for Ian to try him over some cross-country fences away from Ivyleaze. So, in great secrecy, a meeting was arranged at Weston Park, where Ian would try Murphy and Ginny would try Griffin. Janet Plant, the secretary at Weston Park, made the advanced fences available to them. For

Ginny it was the first time she had ridden cross-country since her injury at Badminton, and she was quite nervous about riding a strange horse over big fences. Griffin ran out at an insignficant practice fence, so Ian laughed at her and told her she would have to make it clear who was the boss. After that they got on very well.

Then it was Ginny's and Dot's turn to laugh at Ian, because Murphy was trotting about with his head in the air refusing to accept any contact from Ian's hands. Eventually they got going, and the opportunity to jump some challenging cross-country obstacles gave Murphy the incentive he needed to show his true colours. Ian soon got the 'feel' that had been lacking when he first tried the horse.

So the exchange was agreed. Murphy went back in the box with Ian and Jenny, and Griffin went to Ivyleaze. Jenny was not too pleased; she was sad to lose Griffin, and she did not like the look of Murphy. 'I thought he was the worst horse we'd ever had on the yard. He was so big and heavy-looking, with a long, dippy back.'

Murphy performing his dressage at his first three-day event with Ian at Boekelo, Holland, in 1988, wearing a rubber snaffle. He only needs the serious 'brakes' for the cross-country.

Ginny Leng
I always regretted swapping Murphy. I regretted it from the moment he was loaded into Ian's lorry.

Heather Holgate – Ginny Leng's mother
Parting with Murphy was a very difficult decision for us all. Perhaps Dot and I are too careful. We certainly hated parting with the horse. Maybe it was our one big mistake – who knows?

The plan was to give the horses a three-week trial with their new riders, which would include competing at Witton Castle. Ian had to go to Perthshire to make a video as soon as he got home, so Murphy was given a week's holiday, but before he returned from Perthshire Ginny rang to say she was quite happy with Griffin and ready to do the swap. Ian hadn't even ridden Murphy again at that stage. 'I rushed home the next day to ride him, but I had pretty well made up my mind anyway. So that was it. By the time we took the horses to Witton the swap had already been completed.'

In hindsight it is easy to say that Ginny made a mistake in exchanging Murphy for Griffin, but at the time it seemed to be the best solution. Griffin's track record was excellent: he was an uncomplicated, well-trained advanced horse, ready to progress to the top level. No one could have known at that stage that he would not have the staying ability to cope with championship-length courses, although Ginny had her suspicions. 'I was never convinced that Griffin was an international prospect. He had a slightly with-drawn character, and one felt that he never really enjoyed his job. He just wasn't my sort of person.'

Nevertheless both Ian and Ginny enjoyed a good start with their new horses by coming first and third respectively at their first three-day event after the swap, at Boekelo, in Holland. Ian's victory there was not without incident, however.

'When I took over the ride on Murphy,' explains Ian, 'I thought, "Right, I'm not going to ride him in any of these strong bits. I'll put him in a French bridoon." ' All went well with this plan initially, and Murphy was placed at all five of his initial one-day events with Ian, including a win at Holker Hall and Thirlestane Castle. But at Boekelo things started to get a little out of hand. 'I did actually manage to hold him on the steeplechase in the bridoon, but as the course went on he stood off each fence a little bit further, and by the end he was taking off from almost outside the wings. Even so, I planned to keep him in the bridoon for the cross-country. But then Marjorie Comerford, who was briefing us in the box, told me that my score was needed for the team, so I thought, "Oh dear, I'd better put the Citation on." I think that might have been a mistake because he actually fought me on the cross-country for the first time with that bit in. It has a very severe action.

'He was fine over the first few fences, but in the middle of the course we had to do some tight turns on a track through a wood. Murphy slipped going round a corner and went down on the flat

On the cross-country at Boekelo, soon after Murphy had slipped up on the flat and flung Ian over the ropes.

on his face. He did three on four strides, still pushing with his back legs while his face was on the ground, and I was up his neck. Then he managed to stop himself and, being Murphy, he didn't just stand up, he leapt up with such force that he shot me straight off his neck and I went over the string at the side of the course and landed in the bushes! Luckily, I managed to keep hold of him – otherwise he would have disappeared into the next county – and I swung back into the saddle, but because I'd wasted all that time I thought I'd better get a move on, and that was when I lost control. It was the first time he'd really run away with me. Up until then he had been quite relaxed and soft and in control, but then he went wooden on me and starting jumping against the hand. Although we went clear I didn't really enjoy the second half of the course because I didn't feel things were right.'

Murphy arrived back at the end of the course with a filthy face and a cut lip from his fall, and everyone wondered what on earth had happened to him. The members of the Ground Jury summoned Ian to show them the Citation bit because they were concerned that it may have been the cause of Murphy's bleeding lip, but after examination they agreed that Murphy had just grazed some skin off his lip when he had fallen.

Mark Phillips – trainer and course designer
Murphy is one of the greatest cross-country horses of all time. His power is something that all spectators can appreciate, and as such he is a terrific crowd-pleaser and a horse that people will travel to see.

Show jumping at Gatcombe in 1988, when Murphy finished third. Ian is still using a short whip, which he later discarded altogether.

Presentations at Thirlestane Castle after Ian and Murphy had won the Scottish Championships in 1988. On the left is David Stevenson, director of the Edinburgh Woollen Mill, Ian's sponsors, and in the middle is Rozzi Maitland-Carew, Glenburnie's breeder.

A clear show-jumping round the following day kept Murphy in the lead, with Mark Todd second and Ginny third, so the first major outing had been a success on paper if nothing else.

It was not until the following year (1989) that both riders ran into teething problems. For Ginny it was a fall in Punchestown with Griffin; for Ian a fall at a one-day event at Belton Park. It happened at the new Sunken Circle, where there was room for only one very short stride at the bottom. 'I came in at a slow canter to the rails,' explains Ian, 'and let him jump the rails and bounce down into the bottom, but as he was coming off the bank I said "whoa" with the reins to make him jump short into the bottom. His reaction to that was to jump against my hands, so that he landed in the bottom with only enough room for a bounce, and because we had come in so slowly he hadn't got the impulsion to get up the step the other side. He got his front legs up all right, but his back legs hit the bank and he smacked into the rails; I went pinging over the top of the rails. I think that was the first time he had ever stopped. He actually hurt himself a bit because he banged his stifles on the bank, and it may have taught him a lesson. It certainly taught me a lesson.'

The partnership's first misunderstanding, at Belton Park in 1989. Ian was thrown over the rails as Murphy came down after hitting the bank.

Lorna Clarke
Of all the horses that I have come across Murphy is the one with whom I would have liked to have done a three-day event, just for the sheer thrill of experiencing the sensation of power that he must give to Ian. Whether or not I would have been able to go with him is another matter!

To watch him across country is amazing; to ride him must be something everyone dreams of, but very few would be capable of.

Ian can recall the fall in such detail because he watched it again and again on video. After it happened he was determined to find out what had gone wrong and what he should do to prevent something like that happening in the future. 'He used to stay up to the early hours studying videos of Murphy,' says Jenny. 'Then one day he said that he thought the only way to ride Murphy at a combination was to be brave and give him his head as he came in and leave it to him to sort out the problem.'

The more Ian watched the tapes the more he became convinced that this was the answer. 'I think the reason he launched himself off over the Ski Jump at Badminton was that he was jumping away from Ginny's hands. I don't think he liked being anchored and that was his way of getting away from her. I got the impression that he would weigh up the situation quite clearly as he came into an obstacle and say, "Right, that's the fence; I know what I'm doing," and as long as you didn't interfere he would just get on with it.

'I decided that as long as I came in at the right speed, I would leave his head alone and the rest would be up to him. I got the impression that if I tried to interfere and I put him wrong that's when I was likely to be catapulted out of the plate. Because he is so powerful and athletic he could get himself out of trouble but would probably jump me off in the process. It took me a while to get used to the idea, and I still find it slightly alarming at times, but it seems the best thing to do.'

There was still the problem of general control to be put right. At first Murphy's strength worried Ian because he did not see how a horse could successfully negotiate difficult fences when the rider was not fully in control. As he got to know Murphy better, he began to trust him more, but he never felt that he could really contain Murphy's power until he put him into a cherry roller American gag at the beginning of 1991.

In contrast, Ian had decided to ride Murphy in the French bridoon at their first Badminton together in 1989, a mistake that became all too apparent as soon as Murphy bounded over the first fence on the cross-country. 'He'd been fine on the steeplechase, so I kept him in the French bridoon for the cross-country,' says Ian. 'In those days I still carried a very short stick, not that I ever used it – it wouldn't have done any good anyway – but just because I felt I should always carry a whip. But after I'd jumped the first fence I threw it at the mounted steward.'

On the steeplechase course at Badminton in 1989. Ian is riding Murphy in a French bridoon, and he is carrying a short whip which he later threw to a steward when Murphy ran away with him at the start of the cross-country course.

Ian realised from the start that he was in for a fight, and the only chance he had of holding Murphy was to wrap the reins round his hands and use his whole bodyweight against the horse. This he needed to do, especially near the end of the course where Murphy started to lean on him because he was becoming tired. They went clear, but Ian had not really enjoyed his ride.

However, one consolation was that Murphy had successfully negotiated the Ski Jump. Much to everyone's relief he made no attempt to launch himself off into space as he had done the previous year with Ginny, but instead dropped over the log quite sensibly – clearly having learnt his lesson.

With a show jump down the following day Murphy finished in fifth place, two points behind his stable companion, Glenburnie.

Ginny won the event on Master Craftsman, but Ian's two greys had done well enough to be included on the long-list for the 1989 European Championships. Indeed, Murphy would probably have had his first outing on the British team if he had not injured himself in a freak accident only four weeks before the championships.

'To this day we don't know how it happened,' says Jenny. 'Somehow, while travelling in the box between the gallops at Lambourn and team training at Badminton, Murphy cut his stifle. There hadn't been any crashing or banging on the journey, and we never found anything in the box that he could have cut himself on, but when he came off the lorry at Badminton there was a deep cut, about two inches long, in his stifle.'

The wound was stitched by a local vet, and it was hoped that Murphy would recover from the accident in time to be considered for the championships. But the wound did not heal well. It bled internally and Murphy developed a large haematoma along his tummy and around the top of his stifle (on his off hind).

When Paul Farringdon, the team vet, took out the stitches and Murphy was turned out in the walled garden at Stowell Park – the home of Lord and Lady Vestey, where Ian keeps his horses during the spring season – the wound burst open. 'It was very messy,' says Ian, 'though at least it healed up quite quickly after that.' But by then it was too late. Murphy had already missed at least two weeks' work at a crucial time and there was nothing for it but to turn him out for the rest of the year. So it was Glenburnie who helped the British team to gain their emphatic victory at the European Championships at Burghley in September.

Facing page: *At the Ski Jump in 1989. 'I think I was probably over-cautious here after what had happened to Ginny the previous year,' says Ian. 'You can see that Murphy is just creeping over it.'*

Badminton, 1989. *'Murphy was good at the Lake. He was very confident,' says Ian.*

CHAPTER FOUR

A Silver Lining

1990 was a good year for Murphy but one of mixed fortunes for Ian. It started badly, with a controversial ban for drug abuse, and it ended with further controversy when Ian was eliminated at Burghley for 'excessive pressing of an exhausted horse'; but in the middle of it all he and Murphy won the team and individual silver medals at the World Equestrian Games in Stockholm.

The initial upset stemmed from a positive drug test on Ian's horse, Foxy V, at the Werribee three-day event in Australia the previous October. According to the FEI (International Equestrian Federation) the blood sample taken from Foxy V contained 10.2 micrograms of 'bute'. The permitted level then was 5.0 micrograms (it has since been reduced to 2.0). Ian had given the horse the equivalent of 1 gram on the night after the cross-country because he thought Foxy might have a slightly bruised foot, and he could not understand why the blood sample showed such a high level.

Although the FEI accepted that Ian had not deliberately overdosed Foxy, it nonetheless imposed an unprecedented three-month suspension on him. The announcement was made at the end of March and the ban was due to take effect after Badminton in May, which would have meant Ian missing the World Championships. Having ridden for the British team for the past five years, Ian was bitter about the decision. At the time of the announcement he said: 'I feel I have bust a gut to get where I have and always had the sport's interests at heart. This is like being kicked in the teeth. Everyone is talking about an appeal so that I can compete at the World Championships, but what I want to do is clear my name.'

In view of the lack of security at the stables at Werribee, the FEI did eventually reduce the severity of its punishment by dropping the suspension and instead fining Ian £3000, but the incident left Ian disillusioned. To help take his mind off the affair, Ian had the two greys – Murphy and Glenburnie – to prepare for Badminton in May. Knowing that he still had a problem with Murphy's brakes across country, Ian thought he would try to influence the horse mentally. The plan was ride him at a slow, schooling pace on the cross-country at the spring one-day events in an attempt to condition him not to get excited and silly. Unfortunately it didn't work.

Facing page: *Murphy in an American gag with a Nathe mouthpiece at Kings Somborne in April, 1990. Ian had decided to start the season by taking Murphy very slowly at his one-day events, but the psychology did not work and Murphy still ran away with him at Badminton.*

Glenburnie and Ian waiting to start Phase A, Roads and Tracks, at Badminton in 1990. For three successive years Ian rode both Murphy and Glenburnie at Badminton.

Facing page: *Jumping boldly into the Lake at Badminton in 1990. Ian had swapped back to the Citation bit in the ten-minute box after Murphy had run away with him on the steeplechase.*

Although Murphy was perfectly in control at the one-day events in an American gag, a new bit that Ian was trying out, when he got to Badminton it was different story.

Ian explains: 'When I rode him in the American gag at one-day events I was so well in control that I had the reins in loops most of the time, so I thought I would keep him in that for Badminton, but when I came out of the box there for the steeplechase he was just gone. I lost control over the first fence. The trouble with the American gag is that once a horse gets away from you, you can't steer either. I had to have both hands on one rein in order to turn the corner. It was terrifying. I had no steering and no control.'

The Worcester Avenue, a maximum height fence after the Lake at Badminton in 1990. Murphy is still pulling hard.

Both Jenny Stark and Heather Holgate were watching this performance in disbelief. 'All I could see', recalls Jenny, 'was a white-faced Ian going round with both hands on one rein.'

Ian had already ridden Glenburnie on the cross-country, and had had an unlucky stop coming out of the water, when Glenburnie had stumbled up the bank to the upturned boat. In spite of the stop, however, Glenburnie had finished inside the optimum time, so Ian was reasonably confident that he could make the time on Murphy. He set off quite slowly but gradually gathered speed, so that by the end of the course he was going at a fair pace. However, when he finished he discovered to his horror that he had collected a massive 17.6 penalties. 'I must have just wasted too much time at the beginning of the course, and then didn't make it up,' says Ian.

So with 17.6 penalties to add to Murphy's dressage score, and 20 penalties to add to Glenburnie's, the two horses finished fourteenth and fifteenth, not such a good result as in the previous year, but they were both still in contention for the forthcoming World Championships in Stockholm. This time, though, it was Glenburnie's turn to suffer an injury, leaving Murphy to make his debut on the British team.

The final trial for Stockholm had been at Milton Keynes, where Ian had been in the happy and reassuring position of being the only rider with two horses on the short-list. The following morning he had two lame horses. 'You can never assume you're going to be on the team,' says Ian. 'I get quite neurotic about it. Those trot-ups in front of the selection committee are more nerve-racking than the competition itself.'

Both horses had gone well round the inviting track at Milton Keynes, but the next morning when Glenburnie came out of the stable to trot up he was very lame. Ian realised it was probably the after-effect of an accident Glenburnie had had while schooling at home at Haughhead only a week before Milton Keynes. At the time Ian had decided to give him quite a big jump to sharpen him up as he had not done any competitions for a while. He took him over a 4ft 6in. upright, which he jumped well. However, as he was coming into it for a second time there was a noise in the yard. 'Typical Glenburnie,' recalls Ian, 'he looked up to see what was happening in the yard just as he took off and he caught a pole between his legs and did a somersault in the school. As a result, he banged the top of an old splint on his front leg, but because he was still totally sound afterwards we thought nothing of it. Unfortunately the run at Milton Keynes must have aggravated the splint and also damaged the suspensory ligament around it. So that put him out for the rest of the season.'

Murphy had come out of his stable perfectly sound at 7.30 in the morning the day after his outing at Milton Keynes, but half and hour later, when Ian took him across the park at Badminton to trot him out in front of the selectors, he was hopping behind. 'I couldn't believe it,' says Ian. 'I was in such a panic. First Glenburnie, and now Murphy.' Fortunately both Ian and the selectors realised that it was a minor injury, and Murphy was still put on the list for the Stockholm squad. All that was wrong with him was a sore stifle, the consequence of hitting the easiest fence on the Milton Keynes course.

Ginny and Griffin had also been selected for the Stockholm team, along with Karen Straker (now Dixon) with Get Smart, and Rodney Powell with The Irishman II. The team would be going to the first ever World Equestrian Games, a venture that brought all the equestrian disciplines – show jumping, dressage, three-day eventing, vaulting, driving and endurance riding – to one venue for their respective world championships. For two weeks Stockholm became the Mecca of the horse world, but for Britain's three-day event team the occasion was tinged with disappointment.

Facing page:
Glenburnie in the water at Milton Keynes, 1990. Ian was trying out a new bit – an Elevator – but it did not stop Glenburnie from snatching at the reins.

Murphy and Ian at Milton Keynes, the final trial for the 1990 World Championships. To Ian's horror, both Murphy and Glenburnie were lame the next morning.

The event started well for the British team, particularly for Rodney Powell, whose dressage score of 46.8 left him in fourth place at the start of the speed and endurance. Murphy's test had been good – he scored 52.2 – but not as good as Ian had hoped. A strange incident had disrupted their concentration just before they went into the arena.

'I had been moved through to the ten-minute arena in preparation for my test,' recalls Ian, 'when suddenly someone came running up to me to ask if he could borrow my spurs. Apparently the Austrian rider, Harald Riedl, had been about to start his dressage test when someone had noticed that he was wearing black plastic spurs, which were not allowed.

'So they took off my spurs while I was sitting on Murphy. I eventually got them back but all the fussing, and the eight minute delay while the Austrian rider changed his spurs, slightly mucked up Murphy's work. He had been going brilliantly, but then he just lost the edge. It probably didn't make that much difference – and anyway I couldn't have let the poor Austrian guy be eliminated – but I got a lot of letters afterwards from people saying, "Never lend your spurs again!" '

The British squad were apprehensive about the cross-country. The course, which had been set out in the Royal Park of Djurgarden, close to the centre of Stockholm, was over uneven ground, and was technically demanding. The track was twisty, and constantly changing between uphill and downhill, so that it would be difficult to establish a rhythm. With few let-ups and no open, galloping stretches, it was going to be hard work for horses and riders. It certainly did not seem like the sort of track that would suit Murphy.

By the time Ian, the last to go for the British team, came to ride the cross-country Britain's chances of a team medal were floundering. Karen Straker, the first of the British riders, had had a stop with Get Smart at the Pleasure Pond (a big water complex near the end of the course); Rodney Powell marred an otherwise perfect round with a run out as he came out of the water at the Redoubt of Charles XI, fence five on the course; and then Ginny ran into all sorts of trouble on Griffin. Her problems started with a refusal coming out of the Pleasure Garden Complex, and then, unaccountably, Griffin tried to put his front feet down between the two hedges of the bullfinch – an action that sent his rider crashing to the ground and brought to an end British hopes of a team gold medal.

It was now down to Ian to keep Britain in the running for a team silver or bronze. New Zealand had already established a commanding lead, and the Germans and Americans were well in touch, so Ian needed to go clear and close to the optimum time if Britain was to have any prospect of a medal.

Paul Farringdon – team vet
When I attended the World Championships in Stockholm, I was concerned as to how a big horse like Murphy would travel – there is not much room in those planes. However, he seemed to positively enjoy the experience and arrived in Stockholm in very good fettle. I well remember Ian's attempts to keep the horse under control during his final gallop on the local racetrack, and I thought, as he flew past me, 'Thank God I'm the vet, not the jockey.'

'I had to start off very slowly,' says Ian, 'because I was under instructions to take the long route at the Redoubt of Charles XI, where Rodney had run out. I knew I would have to be in complete control to do the turns for that, so I had probably wasted about twenty seconds by the time I got there, and, because of the nature of the course, it was difficult to make that up. There were so many twists and turns, and ups and downs, that I had to steady Murphy up quite a lot. Even so, I still came into one or two fences faster than I had intended.

'I remember Mark Phillips, who had been briefing us, saying that you always think you are going faster than you are through woods, and that you need to drop your hands on the horse's neck and let him go, and just sit there and let the horse back himself off the trees. There were a lot of tight turns, where we sometimes brushed a tree or I caught my knee. I'd see a tree coming and think, "Help! My shoulder, or my leg." You had to be brave enough to let the horse sort it out, but it was quite frightening. I thought going through the woods at that speed was worse than doing the jumps.'

Murphy made nothing of the obstacles, bounding round the course with enthusiasm and energy, and taking out strides here and there, so that spectators were left gasping in amazement. He seemed to treat the fences with disdain. 'Everyone said he would bounce the Road Crossing – rails followed by a huge hedge with a drop – but I honestly didn't think he would,' says Ian. 'You approached the fence down a hill and had to drop off a stone, and then there was one stride – quite a long stride – to the first rail onto the road. Murphy got a bit long there and just ballooned over the

Taking the quick route into the water complex at Stockholm. Murphy had lost an overreach boot from his near fore.

rails, so that was it; then I knew it was coming. I just thought, "Here we go!"

'Probably the worst thing was that we hit the subsequent fence, the Double Oak. It was a maximum height parallel, but to Murphy it was just a simple fence. I hadn't steadied him much because I had assumed he would back off it a bit, but he didn't, and he hit it very hard. He'd put in such a big effort at the Road Crossing, and I think he slightly lost his concentration after that.'

Karen Dixon (née Straker)
Watching Murphy bounce the Road Crossing in Stockholm was amazing. The second part of the combination, the hedge, was enormous. When we walked the course I stood on the landing side of it with my hands in the air and no one could see me from the other side. When Murphy bounced it we were all watching on the TV monitor in the ten-minute box. The atmosphere was electric.

I find it very interesting to watch Scotty working in before a big competition. He has a very positive attitude and is quite happy to go off for a gallop and a jump, whereas I tend to be thinking of dressage, and nothing but dressage, until I have got that part over with. Ian appears to be bluffing the horse a bit; his approach is just to get on with it, and it seems to relax them both.

Facing page: *At the fourth fence at the World Championships in Stockholm, where Ian was under instructions to take the long route. 'That's where I wasted all my time,' says Ian.*

Lucinda Green
*My image of Murphy is twofold. One is of him running away at Kings
Somborne down the last hill towards the penultimate fence, with Ginny Leng's
diminutive figure unable to make any impression on him. The second is of
Murphy and Ian bouncing, with immense power, the Road Crossing at
Stockholm in 1990, and then flippantly almost crashing through the next
insignificant fence.*

*He is singularly the most powerful horse I have ever seen in my life and he
completely exalts in his power, which makes him incredibly cocky. When I am
teaching I sometimes find myself saying: 'No horse will ever do such and such
unless, of course, he's called Murphy Himself!'*

A lesser horse than Murphy might have come down as a result
of hitting such a big, solid fence, but the grey is so strong and
powerful that, although the impact tipped him forward and Ian
went to the buckle end, the horse was never in danger of falling.
One good thing about his mistake was that it made him pay more
attention to the next obstacle, the Pleasure Pond, where he jumped
well through the left hand side, dropping over the park rails into
the water, then four strides to the Normandy Bank with a rail back
into the water, and then out over the step and rails. It was at the
water complex that many riders had run into trouble. Mark Todd
had had a stop with Bahlua at the rails on the Normandy Bank;
Susanna Macaire, riding as an individual for Britain, had fallen
going into the water, and even Blyth Tait with Messiah, the even-
tual World Champions, very nearly had a refusal here.

There were only seven fences left to jump after the water, but
by now the heat, with temperatures creeping up close to the 90s,
and all the ups and downs and turns, had been taking their toll on
Murphy. Because he is such a big-striding horse and he was travelling quite fast, he was having to make constant adjustments to keep
his balance. If any course was going to take it out of him it was this
one. An open, galloping track like Badminton is much easier for
him.

'I've never really tired Murphy, and I never thought he would
tire,' says Ian, 'but about three fences from the end of the course in
Stockholm it was like pulling the plug. From being a double handful and a struggle to hold he suddenly dropped the bridle and cantered home. He still jumped the fences all right, but I wouldn't have
liked to have jumped anything very big or complex. I had to use a
lot of leg to try to at least keep him on a light contact. It just wasn't
like Murphy at all.'

However, the next morning he had fully recovered. When Ian and Ginny took Murphy and Griffin for a hack before the show jumping, Murphy came out fly-bucking and Griffin was squealing. Murphy then tried to run away with Ian while being trotted up at the final horse inspection.

Murphy's dramatic round on the previous day's cross-country had restored British hopes of a silver or bronze medal and had brought Ian into fourth place individually. The New Zealand team had such an impressive lead that they could afford to have nineteen fences down in the show jumping before losing the gold medal. Britain, on the other hand, was only twelve points ahead of West Germany, so there was little leeway for mistakes. As it turned out, both teams had three fences down, so the positions were unaltered.

Murphy jumped a steady, careful clear round, collecting just 0.25 time penalties, and when New Zealand's Andrew Nicholson and the Frenchman Didier Seguret (lying third and second respectively) both had fences down Ian moved up into the silver medal position. By then, however, the New Zealand rider Blyth Tait had three fences in hand and had little difficulty in securing the World Championship title.

To Ian it seemed that he was fated always to be the runner-up at international championships. At the European Championships in Luhmühlen in 1987 he had won the individual silver medal (with Sir Wattie) and at the Seoul Olympics the following year the same partnership again won the individual silver medal. Now at the 1990 World Championships Ian had become the silver medallist for the third time, and he must have been wondering whether he would ever cast off his second-place jinx. When that time did come – at the 1991 European Championships in Punchestown – it was with Glenburnie, not Murphy, that he gained his European title.

However, before such happier times Ian was to be confronted by further criticism and controversy. It began with some rather cutting comments from Mark Phillips in his *Horse and Hound* column just three weeks after the World Championships. Although Ian knew that he still needed to work on Murphy's control across country, he was surprised by the article. Capt Phillips had written:

'Everybody marvelled at Ian Stark's bravery and Ian Stark the competitor as he launched himself around Stockholm's cross-country course on Murphy Himself. I am a tremendous admirer of Ian the horseman but I did not enjoy watching it.

Mary Thomson
'Boldness', 'ability' and 'sheer power' are the words which spring to mind when asked to describe Murphy Himself. Scotty and Murphy together are an invincible combination, both being real dare devils with nerves of steel.

The final horse inspection at Stockholm, before the show jumping. 'Murphy was so full of himself,' recalls Ian, 'that when I turned him to trot back towards the Ground Jury he set off in a medium trot, dragging me along with him.' A clear show-jumping round gave Ian the individual silver medal.

'Ian would be the first to admit that, although delighted with his silver medal, he would have wished to have won it in a more controlled manner. His round was either going to end up with a medal or a very serious accident. To me it was much too close to the latter.

'Missing out strides and standing off a long way is not good or safe cross-country riding, and Scotty would not want any young or aspiring riders to emulate the way he tackled some of those fences.'

Ian was upset by the comments, not least because it was Capt Phillips who had instructed him to go fast and clear for the team in Stockholm. 'So I went fast,' says Ian, 'slightly out of control at times, but I didn't see how else I could get near the time. I know Murphy sometimes gives the impression of being dangerously close to the edge, but it doesn't feel that way to me. It is his sheer power and scope that make him exciting to watch. It doesn't worry me when he takes out strides, because it is what I have come to expect. I can tell by the way he jumps into a combination exactly what he is going to do as he comes out of it. I just have to stay with him.'

There are few riders who could stay with Murphy when he is bounding around a cross-country course, and Ian has received universal admiration for his ability to do just that. His talent and flair for cross-country riding have always been highly regarded by other riders, few of whom would dare to set out on a horse as powerful as Murphy, so it was not surprising that when Sarah Bullen damaged her collarbone in a fall at Thirlestane Castle she offered Ian the ride on her horse, Alfresco, at Burghley.

Ian took up the opportunity, but was soon to regret it. His cross-country round on Alfresco ended with a bad fall and elimination from the event by the Ground Jury for 'excessive pressing of an exhausted horse.'

Both Ian and Sarah Bullen were stunned by the decision. Alfresco's fall at Lambert's Bed, the penultimate fence, was in their view just unlucky: he had caught his front feet on the top rail and flipped over. Michael Seckington, one of the official vets at Burghley, attended the horse and was quite satisfied that he was merely winded and not exhausted. Indeed, Alfresco was soon up on his feet and dragging his owner back to the stables, where he tucked into his supper with relish, and the next morning he was perfectly sound.

Ian, on the other hand, was far from fit and well. He had been taken to hospital immediately after the fall, where they put a collar on his neck. He had aggravated a bad back injury sustained the previous year when he had a fall with a novice called Set Sail at Charterhall.

Further injury of the kind he suffered at Burghley was not going to do his career prospects any good, but more damaging than that was the effect of the Ground Jury's decision on Ian's already battered self-esteem. The elimination itself was difficult enough to accept, but it was the way that it was done that upset Ian most. As Jenny explains: 'I brought him back from the hospital at about 10pm, and as we drove back into Burghley Park someone told us that we had to go and see the stable manager. It took us a while to track him down, but eventually we found him in the canteen, where he handed Ian an envelope. Inside was a statement of the Ground Jury's decision. No one had spoken to Ian, or had tried to interview him to find out his version of events, and no one had bothered to wait and explain the decision to him. It was just there in the envelope. It was so impersonal.

'Ian couldn't believe it. It was the final straw as far as he was concerned. He'd been given two suspensions within six months, neither of which he felt was justified. That night he made up his mind to give up eventing.

'It took a lot of persuasion to keep him going. I never wanted him to give up. It was just one of those completely unfortunate incidents. One of the things about being in the sport at this level is that you have to cope with terrible disappointments as well as success, and you have to keep going. But Ian felt very harassed by it all, and it took him a long time to get over it. When we got home we did have one hate-mail type of letter, which was really nasty, but on the whole people were very supportive, and we had a lot of nice letters which I think helped Ian get back on his feet.'

The enforced rest to recover from his injury gave Ian time to plan the following season's campaign. He was well aware that something still needed to be done about Murphy's attitude to his cross-country, otherwise the horse might just take one liberty too many and land himself in trouble. The control with the Citation bit was reasonable, but Ian had never been very happy with it because it hurt Murphy's mouth and he felt that the horse was sometimes running away from the pain. He had persevered with the bit because he hadn't found anything better, but during the autumn after Stockholm, while rummaging around in a tack shop, Ian came across something called a cherry roller American gag. The following spring he decided to try it out on Murphy.

CHAPTER FIVE

The Ride of a Lifetime

Once the spring season gets under way Ian and Jenny bring some of their horses down to Stowell Park, in Gloucestershire, the home of Lord and Lady Vestey, where they base themselves until Badminton is over. They first came down here in 1987 when Ian was preparing Sir Wattie for Badminton, which was later cancelled because of torrential rain.

'It was very much thanks to Henrietta Knight, who was chairman of the selectors' committee at the time, that we got this wonderful opportunity,' explains Jenny. 'She had suggested to Ian that her sister, Lady Vestey, might be able to put us up for the spring season.

'It was quite an adventure. We uprooted the kids from school, packed up most of our belongings and about ten horses, and moved. Our friends at home thought we had left Scotland for good.'

The children, Stephanie and Tim, now go to a weekly boarding school near to the Stark's home at Ashkirk, so they are not disrupted by the annual migration, but it is still a major feat of organisation to move the main Stark establishment down south for the spring season. Jenny finds herself commuting between Gloucestershire and Scotland to keep up with her husband and her children.

Preparations for Badminton 1991 went well, with Murphy going happily in his new bit. He came second at Belton Park one-day event and first at Brigstock. 'Instead of preparing him slowly at

---

Lady Vestey

It is fun for everyone here at Stowell Park when the Stark entourage moves in for the spring season. Murphy pulls faces when you talk to him over the stable door. He likes to look fierce, but one can always get round that with a packet of Polos.

My favourite memory of Murphy was in 1991 when, on the Tuesday before Badminton, we took the two greys for their last proper piece of work up Compton Cassey (which is a part of Stowell with a brilliant hill for galloping). We cantered along the valley upsides, with me on Glen, and then turned up the hill, whereupon Glen accelerated away from Murphy, and Murphy, in a bait, pulled up. We thought there must be something wrong with him, but four days later he virtually won Badminton!

Passing the judges' boxes before starting their dressage test at Badminton in 1991. The test was one of the best that Murphy has ever produced, but it was marked with unexpected severity.

the start of the season, as I had done the previous year,' explains Ian, 'I wanted to get him used to going at the correct speed so that he wouldn't take off when he got to a three-day event. So we went fast at the one-day events, but I was still in control because I had him in the new bit. It was working well on Murphy because the cherry rollers stopped him from leaning on the bit, and if he tried to take off I had enough control with the gag action to be able to stop him, yet the bit didn't seem to hurt him in the way that the Citation had.'

Hugh Thomas – Director of Badminton Horse Trials

Murphy's spectacular jumping has made him a byword among course designers and technical delegates worldwide. We all have to be careful to avoid fences that are only suitable for Murphy. I well remember standing with Tommy Brennan in the summer of 1991 at one of his magnificent Punchestown fences before it was finished, discussing how Murphy would jump it. The conclusion, of course, was 'very easily', but we agreed that others might not manage it quite so well.

Murphy looking lean and fit during his dressage test. In preparation for Badminton Ian had taken Murphy much faster on the cross-country at one-day events.

At Badminton on Thursday morning Murphy produced an excellent dressage test despite the blustery weather and a mistake by his jockey, who, riding the new FEI test for the first time, took the wrong course. But Murphy's marks were a disappointment. Jane Pontifex wrote in her report in *Horse and Hound*: 'Murphy produced one of the best tests of his career, powerful but controlled, floating over the ground with smooth transitions between well-marked paces. Though he finally lost patience when trotting up the centre line to the closing salute, it looked an impressive performance. The judges, however – Dr Springorum, Mrs Isobel Reid and Count Pocci – were not so impressed and they marked it with unexpected severity.'

Mark Holliday –
groom to Ian Stark
*It's an amazing
feeling to be grooming
for Murphy at a
competition knowing
that he is one of the
best eventers in the
world. I get a
tremendous thrill out
of it. He is a very
easy horse to look
after, and although he
sometimes pulls faces
at people, he's
actually very sweet in
the stable.*

*He does worry quite
a lot, especially before
a big event. He's got
the timetable for
Badminton worked
out now. A week
before the event starts
he goes there to be
shod; then he knows
what's happening and
starts to count down
the days. He won't
eat a scrap of hard
feed until he arrives at
his stable at
Badminton, two days
before the event
begins. Then he
relaxes and eats a
phenomenal amount.
All the tension and
waiting are over, and
he knows he's there to
do a job.*

His score of 52.2 left him in fourth place after the dressage, but with Mary Thomson and King Boris out in front on 44.4, Murphy and Ian had quite a lot of ground to make up. Unfortunately Glenburnie's test had been even more disappointing, resulting in a score of 62.2, so that even if he went well across country he was unlikely to be in serious contention for first place.

The day before the speed and endurance, Ian took Murphy for a quiet hack along the roads and tracks to the airfield. 'I started to canter him along the airfield and he was fine,' says Ian, 'so I thought I would just open him up a bit, and he suddenly went from a very controlled, steady canter to a runaway gallop down the airstrip. When we reached the bottom I couldn't stop him because I had him in a rubber snaffle, so I had to turn him in huge circles to pull him up.

'I then tried to hack him quietly back to the park, but he was so excited that my attempts to get him to walk were doomed – he fly-bucked all the way to the entrance of the park. Standing by the fence at one of the gates was a group of Animal Rights people with a big placard saying: "Animal Abusers Compete Here". So I said to the man on the gate: "What about abuse to humans by horses?" '

The following day Murphy set out on Phase A (roads and tracks) and settled well. Ian wasn't sure how he would behave on the steeplechase, because it was the first time he had ridden him in the cherry roller American gag at a three-day event. Fortunately Murphy seemed to be in one of his relaxed moods as they set off from the start box, and he accepted the contact without pulling.

Murphy never wants to walk on Phase C – he likes to keep jogging – so Ian finds it best to let him trot on slowly. When they arrived at the ten-minute box Murphy was still feeling relaxed, whereas Ian's nerves were beginning to jangle a little. His daughter, Stephanie, had been in the competitors' marquee watching the television monitor, and had seen Anne-Marie Evans, the first to go on the cross-country, come down the Beaufort Staircase with Tombo. She had put in a stride at the bottom of the steps, hit the palisade and fallen off. So Stephanie came running out of the tent shouting: 'Dad, Dad, Anne-Marie's had a fall at the Beaufort Staircase, so you'll have to bounce the bottom.' 'Thank you, Stephanie!' was Ian's response to his daughter's encouraging pronouncement.

All boded well. Murphy, fourth to go, did not bottle himself up when he went into the start box, as he often does. He set out at a good pace without charging off and pulling Ian into the first fence. Added to this, Ian felt that the cross-country course, which was big and challenging, and favoured the bold but accurate horses, was ideal for Murphy. With the grey's power now better harnessed, Ian was in for the ride of a lifetime.

'Murphy is a law unto himself and one of the great personalities of our time,' wrote Mark Phillips in his *Horse and Hound* commentary after Badminton. 'When he enters the start box there is almost a hushed air of expectancy and we were not to be disappointed. Never can such a big track have been made to look so small and treated with such disdain.'

Starting out over the Whitbread Barrels and the Lamb Creep, Murphy then jumped boldly at the Pheasant Feeder and then out over the Huntman's Brush before a tight turn to the Ha-Ha Rails.

Fence 5, the Ha-Ha Rails.

'There was a slight bump in front of the rails,' explains Ian, 'but rather than taking off from the top of the bump, which would have meant standing off a mile, Murphy went over the lip and in close to the ditch before taking off, so then I knew he wasn't thinking of trying to run away with me. His whole attitude seemed to have changed in response both to the new bit, which he didn't fight against, and to the way I had trained him that season by getting him accustomed to going at a faster pace at his one-day events. I also think he may have learnt a lesson from Stockholm, where for the first time in his life, he tired himself out on the cross-country.'

The only serious mistake Murphy made on the entire thirty-fence course was at the next fence, the Quarry. He jumped in well, over the left-hand side of the wall, and then Ian took him straight on to jump the large log pile on the lip of the quarry. Surprisingly, Murphy put in an extra stride going up the bank and hit the log

pile hard with his front feet. But, as in Stockholm, where he hit the big parallel, he did not fall.

After the Quarry came the run down to the Keeper's Oxer, the sort of fence Murphy loves because the huge ditch makes him back off a little and then he powers over the rails. 'That's when you feel "Wow! This is some horse," ' says Ian. 'He can stand off and jump two or three feet above the fence and way out the other side of it, and you get the most wonderful feeling.'

Next was the Little Badminton S, a zig-zag rail sited on very uneven ground. Ian was one of the few riders to take the straight route here, but Murphy came in a little close to the rails. 'Although I had seen where I wanted to take off,' says Ian, 'the bumps altered Murphy's stride and he ended up burying himself in front of the fence. I thought he might hit it because it was such an upright rail, but he didn't touch it. He just went straight up like a helicopter and got himself out of trouble.

Facing page: Ian and Murphy at the Quarry during their memorable Badminton ride in 1991. 'This was controlled power of the magnitude we may never see again,' wrote Mark Phillips.

Over the Keeper's Oxer. 'It is the sort of fence Murphy loves,' says Ian. 'He just powers over the rails, and that's when you feel "Wow! This is some horse." '

Near right: *Into the
Lake. Murphy always
jumps very boldly into
water, sometimes
catching Ian unawares
so that he gets slightly
left behind. 'When that
happens it's always my
right arm that goes!'
says Ian.*

'Then came the fence that worried me most – the Beaufort
Staircase. There was a big, upright palisade at the top of the staircase and only a narrow platform on which to land before dropping
down the three big steps. I was worried that Murphy would over-
jump and miss the top step completely, so I was very conscious of
giving him the rein to make sure he just dropped down on the
other side of the palisade and didn't jump out too far. I approached
at a very slow canter and got him in as close as I could and then
gave him total freedom of his head so that he jumped in a rounded
way instead of jumping out.

*Fence 10, the Beaufort
Staircase.*

'I knew as we came down the steps that there was no way he
would put.in a stride at the bottom before the second palisade. He
was so sharp and so quick coming down the staircase that he just
touched down after the bottom step and took off again. It felt as if
that was exactly what you were meant to do.'

The Whitbread Drays were quite close to the Lake this time,
which suited Ian because he could steady Murphy back for the
Drays and then keep him moving slowly to the Lake without wasting time trying to pull him up again. Murphy bounced over the two

Fences 12–13, the Lake.

Above: *Jumping the arrowhead, the most direct route, at Henry's Corner. The picture on page 2 shows Murphy at the same fence, but is taken from a different angle.*

sets of white rails into the water as if he was doing a schooling exercise – a little gymnastic grid work. 'He made nothing of it,' says Ian. 'When we landed in the water I was thinking, "Have we really jumped that?"'

'Although Murphy is a big, heavy horse to look at, he lands very lightly over a fence and stretches his front legs well out ahead of him, so when he jumps into water you don't come to a grinding halt. He touches down in the water, absorbs the impact and then he's up for the next stride straight away, so you don't lose your balance.'

The Bullfinch was the next obstacle after the Lake – a 4ft 6in. hedge with nearly a 6-foot spread. Murphy came up the hill on a good stride and gave Ian a lovely jump over it. Then there was the Coffin, which was easier this time because the rails had been set further back from the ditch. Murphy put in a quick stride either side of the ditch, but because he is so nimble Ian hardly knew he had done it.

The Irish Bank caused no problems, and at Henry's Corner Ian took the direct route over the arrowhead. There then followed the Vicarage Vee, another fence demanding pinpoint accuracy, but for Murphy and Glenburnie it is the sort of obstacle that they jump quite happily. 'As long as you have a good line and you are riding forward, the horses don't really notice the ditch, and their natural jump will take them beyond the ditch anyway,' explains Ian.

Fence 17, Henry's Corner.

At the Vicarage Pond, a new water fence, both Murphy and Glenburnie jumped boldly over the maximum-height rails into the water. 'It was a jolly big fence,' says Ian. 'You were landing straight into the water, so there was quite a drop. Murphy got in a little closer than I had intended, but it didn't seem to bother him.

When they came to the Luckington Lane Bank, Ian was aware that Murphy did a tremendous jump over it, but he did not realise just how dramatic it had been until he saw a video showing an aerial view of his performance. 'I came in at an angle to avoid wasting time and I let him approach a bit faster than I would on most horses, so instead of jumping onto the bank, taking a small stride and jumping off, Murphy jumped onto the top of the bank and bounced straight off again over the rail. That bank has a big arch anyway, and taking it at quite a severe angle made it even bigger.

'I checked my watch after the Luckington Lane crossing and I

Fence 20, Luckington Lane Bank.

was slightly down on time. I didn't kick on, but I did just let him open up a bit, so he was travelling quite fast by the time we reached the Centre Walk. He didn't feel out of control – he hadn't felt out of control all the way – he just felt powerful. He stood off the first brush and landed so far out into the road that I remember thinking I would just have to keep going and stand off the next one as well, but I didn't realise it was only going to be *two* strides!'

Most horses put in four strides between the two Centre Walk hedges. In 1990 Glenburnie and Murphy both did it in three. 'I thought that was quite something,' says Ian, 'but when Murphy did it in two it felt perfectly normal. You didn't get the impression that he was having to reach for it, which just shows how long his stride must be – about twice the length of a normal event horse.'

In previous years when Murphy had opened up over the Centre Walk hedges Ian had had a serious problem getting him back under control again to jump Tom Smith's Wall. This time, however, he came back quite quickly and jumped the corner accurately.

Two years ago at the Second Luckington Lane Crossing Murphy had bounced between the two hedges across the road, where the distance was 24ft 6in – a long stride for a double. So people were joking that Murphy would bounce the crossing again, but Ian took the quick route over the angled rail to the hedge. 'There's no way we could have bounced that. It was such an angle,' says Ian.

He was still down slightly on the clock and it was tempting to let Murphy go faster at this stage. The next fence was the Footbridge, which was quite straightforward, but after that came the Wayside Inn, which involved either a bounce or a right-angled corner. It was a single rail corner, which demanded considerable accuracy, and Ian didn't dare let Murphy go until they had jumped it. He did it well, never waivering off his line; then Ian let rip for home.

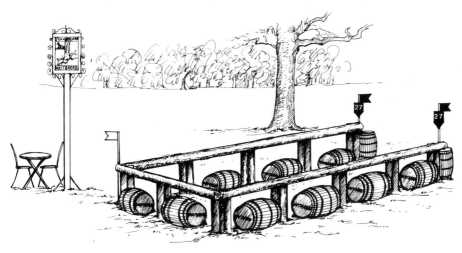

Fence 27, the Wayside Inn.

'The nice thing was that, having jumped the third and second from the last fences fast and a little bit flat, and then galloped all the way past the front of the house, Murphy still came right back to me for the turn to the Whitbread Bar, so he really was in control all the way. We finished the course with just a couple of time faults, and in hindsight I realise that I could have done the time easily because I could have let him go on a bit faster without being in danger of losing control.'

The only rider who did finish the course within the optimum time was Rodney Powell on The Irishman, and by the end of the speed and endurance he was less than three points behind Ian. Murphy's brilliant cross-country round had taken Ian into the lead, and another good round from his stable companion, Glenburnie, had put Ian in fifth place as well.

Murphy is usually a careful, reliable show jumper, but at Badminton that year things went wrong. Ian jumped Glenburnie clear and then did a quick swap to Murphy, who was the last horse to jump. 'I think I was slightly hurrying myself as I leapt off Glen and onto Murphy, and that probably rubbed off on him. In my haste I forgot that I was still carrying my whip, which Murphy hates. The atmosphere in the arena was incredibly buzzy, and as we went in people cheered. I think the combination of all those things blew Murphy's brains. He cantered into the arena and halted quite happily, but then as we went to move off he started to bottle up and I thought, "Crikey, here we go!" '

Struggling to keep control, Ian looked as if he might just pull it off, but then Murphy knocked down the triple bar, one of the easiest fences on the course. 'It wasn't the fence that was the problem,' says Ian. 'It was Murphy's state of mind.' Rodney Powell had already jumped clear on The Irishman, leaving Ian no room for error, so when the triple bar came down it brought an end to Murphy's chances of winning his first Badminton title.

For Ian the disappointment of dropping to second place was partly off-set by the knowledge that Murphy had given him the best cross-country ride round Badminton that he has ever had on any horse. 'It gave me the most wonderful feeling because instead of coming into fences trying to steady him I could just keep coming in a rhythm.' There had been no fighting; everything had looked natural and effortless, even when he had taken out strides. As Mark Phillips wrote: 'This was controlled power of the magnitude we may never see again.'

The two greys on parade at Badminton before the start of the show jumping.

Murphy show jumping, before he knocked down the triple bar and ended his chance of winning his first Badminton title.

Murphy with all four feet off the ground during his explosive show-jumping round. He is looking quite happy, while Ian, who has now dropped the whip that he was inadvertently carrying, is very worried.

Murphy looking pleased with himself at the prize-giving, standing in front of John Hills, the chief steward at Badminton, alongside the winners, Rodney Powell and The Irishman. 'Judging by the look on his face you'd think it was Murphy who had won, not The Irishman,' says Ian.

CHAPTER SIX

Glenburnie Steals the Limelight

Ian was brought straight back down the earth the day after Badminton when Murphy was found to be slightly lame. Fortunately, he recovered within twenty-four hours, so there seemed little cause for concern. He was rested for a few weeks, and then came back into work for the Auchinleck one-day event at the end of July, where he ran well. However, the day after the event he was lame again, this time for two days. It is unusual for Murphy ever to be lame so Ian spoke to the selectors about it and to Paul Farringdon, the team vet. Ian's view was that Murphy should not run at Gatcombe, where they were holding the final trial for European team selection, but Paul Farringdon felt that if there was problem it ought to be identified at Gatcombe, rather than waiting until they got to the championships.

So Murphy ran at Gatcombe, where he finished sixth, and was perfectly sound afterwards. 'I thought it must have been nothing and that I could ignore it,' says Ian, 'but after he'd been on the gallops during team training he was lame again for two days. There was obviously something wrong, so we took him to Lambourn to have his bones and tendons scanned. All they could find was a small inflammation in his fetlock joint, and it was thought that he had probably twisted his fetlock at Badminton and that he hadn't had a long enough rest afterwards. Unfortunately we hadn't been aware that there was a serious problem as he was only lame for a day.'

The scans had also revealed two boney spurs in front of the fetlock joint that could be aggravating the inflammation, and pin-firing was recommended to break up the bone. Although the vets at Lambourn were impressed by how clean Murphy's legs were, considering the mileage he had done, they took the view that if the spurs were left without treatment then arthritis might set in, and Murphy would have, at the most, one season left in eventing. 'I didn't have any particularly strong views on firing,' says Ian, 'but I wasn't happy about Murphy being fired because I felt he didn't owe me anything. On the other hand, he wouldn't find retirement easy because I don't think he'd be much good at anything else other than eventing. So in the end I decided that, for his sake as

Murphy convalescing at Phoebe Stewart's farm after his pin-firing operation in 1991. The marks from the operation can be seen on his lower forelegs.

much as anything, it would be right to have the leg fired.'

With Murphy recuperating at Lambourn it was Glenburnie's turn to steal the limelight, and he certainly made the most of his opportunity. Although the Irish were bitterly disappointed not to see Murphy compete over a track that was thought to be ideally suited to him, Glenburnie's cross-country round at Punchestown lacked none of the drama and excitement that spectators of the sport have come to associate with Ian's riding. In 'Memorable Moments of 1991 Sport' in the *Independent*, Genevieve Murphy wrote the following:

'You could not help but be thrilled by the brave and headstrong Glenburnie as he tackled those awesomely solid fences. And, as he threatened to dictate a pace that could have proved suicidal, you had to be lost in admiration for the courage of the man who dared to ride such a tearaway.

'There was one moment when Stark let the horse stride on. The burst of power and speed that was thus unleashed would have been worthy of Glenburnie's racehorse sire, Precipice Wood, who won the 1970 Ascot Gold Cup.

'There had been much disappointment in Ireland when Murphy Himself, Stark's other ebullient partner, went lame. The understudy proved just as exciting.'

Facing page: Glenburnie at Thirlestane Castle, where he went to rest after the European Championships in Punchestown.

Glenburnie –
Badminton, 1991.

Glenburnie's role as 'understudy' had begun in the days when Ian was still competing with Sir Wattie. He came second to Sir Wattie at Badminton in 1988, and although Sir Wattie was Ian's first choice for the Olympics that year, Glenburnie ruled out any chance he might have had of going to Seoul by injuring himself during team training. So Sir Wattie helped Ian to gain his individual and team Olympic silver medal, after which he was retired. At that point Glenburnie might justifiably have expected to become Ian's number-one horse, but then Murphy arrived on the scene.

Although Glenburnie managed to better the young upstart at Badminton the following year, and he also helped the British team to a gold medal at the subsequent European Championships (1989), Murphy's extravagant action and flamboyant cross-country performances have tended to overshadow Glenburnie's own, considerable, talents.

Facing page: *Ian and Glenburnie at the Stick Pile, the penultimate fence at Badminton in 1991, when they finished sixth.*

Bred out of a Thoroughbred mare called Maytime and by Precipice Wood, Glenburnie had been destined for the racetrack, but when the horse was sent to Haughhead as a four-year-old for a few lessons, his future – as far as Ian was concerned – was to be in eventing. 'I tried to buy him then, but his owners, Bunny and Rozzi Maitland-Carew, wouldn't sell him. Eventually, when he was six, they let me take him to an event, and a few months later the Edinburgh Woollen Mill, who had just begun sponsoring me, bought Glenburnie for me to ride.'

Although there was no doubting Glenburnie's ability to jump, his dressage left much to be desired. 'Glen is not blessed with a good trot,' say Ian. 'As a young horse he didn't have a proper working trot and he didn't know anything about lengthening. He just stuck his head in the right position and scuttled around like a demented mouse.' His temperament did not help, because he was so inattentive, which made training difficult. Even now Ian has to work very hard on getting him settled enough for his dressage.

So in Punchestown Ian gave him a tremendous amount of work the day before his test. He rode him out for an hour and quarter in the morning, then did some schooling. In the afternoon he did another forty-five minutes' exercising, and that evening galloped him three times round the practice dressage field. Later on the same evening he took him out again and lunged him on a good patch of grass that he had located between the sale ring (where a big horse sale was in progress) and the polo field (where a game was in progress). After about threequarters of an hour Glenburnie eventually got bored with whizzing round on the end the lunge and he put his head down and relaxed. Contented that he had finally given in, Ian put him back in his stable for the night. 'The trouble with Glenburnie is that he gets himself so fit that he then needs lots of work before he'll settle down,' explains Ian.

The following morning Glenburnie produced the test of a lifetime. Calm, relaxed, and benefiting from going early in the day when there were fewer people around, Glenburnie was a reformed character. His score of 47.4, the best result he has ever achieved, put Ian into fourth place after the dressage. In the lead at this stage was another British team member, Mary Thomson with King William, and in second place was Karen Straker with Get Smart.

The previous day's work and the relatively quiet atmosphere had clearly helped Glenburnie, but Ian also attributes his improved dressage to some homeopathic treatment the horse had recently been undergoing. It had all started at the beginning of the year when Glenburnie was out walking. 'We had been out for about an hour with some of the other horses,' recalls Ian, 'when suddenly, for no reason, he started running backwards, and then sideways, and then he ran into a ditch and spent about a minute digging holes in it. I thought he'd gone crazy.

'The vet came to look at one of our other horses soon after we got back from exercising so I asked him how you would know if a horse had a brain tumour. He said, "Well, you shoot him and then have a look!" I didn't think Glen would appreciate that. However, our vet did put us onto another vet in the area who specialises in homeopathy, so I rang her up and explained what had happened and she sent me some homeopathic pills for Glen. Now he takes these all the time while he is working and he is a different horse. He used to get uptight and naughty, and sometimes he'd just go over the top and have a temper tantrum. When he got very angry there was nothing you could do with him. These pills (he takes a dose of Belladonna and Lysine) seem to help him relax, and the nice thing about them is that they're legal!'

Lucinda Green

Glenburnie is a very classy horse. One moment I will always recall was at Punchestown in 1991 when Ian put his foot down to gain time on a galloping piece of the cross-country two-thirds of the way round. I don't think I have ever seen a horse gallop so fast at that stage of an arduous CCIO, but Glenburnie's head bored down lower and lower as Ian tried to slow him and re-balance him for the next fence. Watching, you knew a battle of strength was on, and it was unnerving to feel that Glenburnie might just win it. He did not, fortunately, but Ian finished utterly exhausted.

With three British riders in the top four places after the dressage in Punchestown, the British team went into the lead ahead of Germany, but such was the influence of the speed and endurance test that the dressage scores were ultimately of little significance. The combined effect of the big, imposing cross-country obstacles, which offered no let-ups; of the taxing steeplechase phase (run over full-size racing fences on a track with a long, uphill pull); and of 16,000 metres of roads and tracks in hot weather took its toll on the horses. By the end of the competition only three of the original ten teams were left in contention.

The British had had a field day. Apart from an unlucky fall into the water for Mary Thomson, which left her nursing a painful

A misty morning for the final horse inspection in the arena at Punchestown. Ian had two show-jumping fences in hand to secure the individual gold medal.

Clearing the Shamrock in the show jumping. Ian had found a four-leaf clover while walking the steeplechase and had kept it inside his hat throughout the event.

Facing page: *Jumping the Irish Spring, fence 19, on their way to victory at the European Championships in Punchestown. Ian had thrown down his whip at the previous obstacle, the Newgrange complex, because Glenburnie was proving such a handful.*

torn ligament in her knee, all had gone well for the team. It started with an inspiring round by Richard Walker on Jacana, who made the daunting course look easy. Then followed Karen Straker, who, despite a refusal at the first water complex, still finished in third place at the end of the cross-country, and then came Ian's brilliant round on Glenburnie which set the seal on Britain's victory. Ian, Richard and Karen all went clear in the following day's show jumping to win, respectively, the gold, silver and bronze individual medals, as well as the team gold. Ian had at last achieved his ambition of winning an individual championship title and had put paid to his 'runner-up' jinx.

Lap of honour time for Glenburnie. A winner at last!

CHAPTER SEVEN

Training and Competing

When Murphy first arrived at Ian and Jenny's home near Ashkirk in Scotland it was clear that Ginny had already done an excellent job in training the horse, and, as far as his dressage was concerned, Ian felt that there was not a lot he needed to do. 'I got the impression that he was a bit bored with dressage, so I didn't do much with him to start with. He was already very obedient and correct, so it was really a question of getting to know him and building up a partnership.

'Although I had ridden other people's advanced horses I had never taken on, as a long-term prospect, a horse as experienced as Murphy. Normally I wouldn't do that because you're just taking on someone else's problems, and there is always the danger that the horse won't adapt to your way of riding. But with Murphy it was different. I knew that he would have been well trained by Ginny and that therefore he would stay on a line when jumping and be accurate, which is what I expect of my own horses.'

Since Ian first began eventing his two bay horses, Oxford Blue and Sir Wattie, he has had help with his dressage from Barbara Slane-Fleming, who lives in Northumberland, about an hour's drive from the Stark's home. She comes over to Haughhead two or three times during the season to look at the horses and help Ian with any problems. She regards Murphy as the most talented horse she has ever come across in over fifty years of teaching.

'He is what I would call a free spirit,' she says. 'You can't boss him about. You just have to accept what he'll do. All the time you are saying to him, "Look, you'd be the greatest if you'd do it this way." You can't really insist on him doing anything, you just have to try to convince him that it would be much better if he did do things your way.

'You can't work Murphy for long periods because he doesn't like to be disciplined for too long. I think that's why Murphy and Ian suit each other; Ian doesn't much like dressage anyway, so for him ten or fifteen minutes is plenty, and it is for Murphy as well. The problem with event horses is that once they know the movements it is very difficult to keep them sweet and really wanting to do the work.

Barbara Slane-Fleming – trainer
In all my years of teaching – from the age of seventeen to seventy-one – I have never come across a horse like Murphy. He is unique. He has got so much character and so much ability, you just can't compare him with any other horse.

Murphy and Ian jumping a corner at Belton Park in 1992.

'It has been largely a psychological thing, coping with Murphy's character. Although on the whole is he a very calm horse, he can blow his top so easily. He's great fun to work with, but he can also be very frustrating sometimes.'

Murphy's complex nature has always been difficult to handle, and even now Ian feels he doesn't fully understand the horse. 'He's so bright that he knows he can always get the upper hand physically, so you have to outwit him and work round things. It's no good going for all-out confrontation. I think if I did that it would be the end of the partnership.'

'Sometimes he seems to sense when he has pushed my patience too far and he'll suddenly show a flash of brilliance. I've always known that you cannot train all horses along similar lines, but I've never had to adapt to a horse as much as I have to Murphy. You need an agreement between a horse and rider and I have had to meet Murphy half way.'

When Murphy is being exercised at home he is usually led from another horse. 'We started doing that because I got sick of riding a lunatic out hacking,' says Ian. 'I think as he's got older he has become more quirky and difficult. He never bucks, but he does this awful bottling up and fly-bucking, which is like a plunge into the air, a very powerful jump into nothing. He'll do a few of those in a row until he's got into overdrive, and then he's built up so much speed that you can't get him anchored. That's how he finds it easiest to run away with you.

Jenny, Ian's wife, riding Glenburnie and leading Murphy while exercising at Stowell Park, where the Starks base themselves for the spring season. Jenny does hours of slow fittening work with the horses.

Working in the school at Haughhead, Scotland. 'Murphy is not fully clipped out until his first spring event because it is usually so cold at home,' says Ian.

'When I am going to do some canter work with any of my other horses,' explains Ian, 'I usually hack quietly up the hill behind our house, jump a couple of gates, cross the road and then go into a big field on our neighbour's farm to canter. Then I walk the horse home again. After Murphy had been up there a couple of times he knew exactly where he was going, and the nearer we got to the gallops the more difficult he became to ride, fly-bucking and trying to run away with me. And then after we'd cantered he wouldn't walk home, he'd start fly-bucking again. After a while I decided that this was getting out of hand, so now, even though the gallops are only half a mile up the road, we put him in the horsebox, take him to the field, gallop him, put him back in the box and take him home again. We are really just trying to avoid a situation where I would get into a fight with him.'

Sometimes Ian will let the students ride Murphy in the school at Haughhead so that they can experience the horse's enormous stride. 'He feels quite different from any other horse,' says Ian. 'The rhythm is so slow because he has got such a big movement. When you are doing rising trot, for example, there is almost a moment of suspension for the rider – everything seems to be in slow motion – and you can feel out of control just cantering across a field simply because of the power beneath you and because of his big stride.'

In the winter Murphy is roughed off and goes out in a field at Phoebe Stewart's farm, about four miles away. Ian likes the horses to be out of sight of the yard so that they can get away from the competition atmosphere and have a proper mental as well as physical break. With Murphy's best friend Glenburnie wintering with the Maitland-Carews at Thirlestane Castle, Murphy is left to fend for himself – something at which he is not very good.

'He's the biggest whimp in the field,' says Ian. 'Phoebe puts five or six horses out in a 30-acre field, and when the weather's bad they get fed twice a day. Murphy won't come near the food until the others are all eating. He waits until the end, and Phoebe has to stand beside him while he eats because if any of the others finish and come towards him he runs away. One winter he was so badly bullied by one of our three-year-olds that we had to take the youngster out of the field. You tend to think of Murphy as being a big, macho hero, but he's actually a bit wet.'

Sheep are no problem, however. When Murphy was at Ivyleaze with Ginny he was sometimes turned out for the winter at Moysie Barton's farm at Shrewton. If any of the sheep in his field got in the way while he was grazing he would pick them up by the scruff of the neck and toss them to one side.

At the beginning of each season, when Murphy is at home at Haughhead and has done plenty of fittening work, he will be looking well conditioned, even a little fat, but any hope of maintaining that condition during the season evaporates as soon as Murphy travels south for his first competition. 'I don't think he really worries about travelling,' says Jenny. 'He just gets excited because he knows what's going on. The weight drops off, especially over his loins and flank, which accentuates his long, dippy back.'

Once Murphy arrives at an event he usually settles in quite happily. He knows the routine so well. Ian can do dressage in a rubber snaffle and show jump him in quite a mild bit without any danger of Murphy trying to run away. It is only when it comes to the cross-country that the serious brakes need to be applied. As soon as Murphy is tacked up with his cherry roller American gag, he begins to shake. He knows exactly what is coming next, and the excitement is almost too much.

Ferdi Eilberg – team dressage trainer
Murphy is a horse who is very much his own character. He has a very big natural movement, which is impressive and, in a way, unusual for an event horse, but when it gets too big without the rider's consent, it can become difficult to make him smooth in the transitions and to keep a good enough balance. Ian has had to work on trying to bring Murphy more together, but without restricting him so much that he would then try to free himself and become inconsistent. It is a question of finding the balance.

Both Glenburnie and Murphy are great fighters. They will always try across country to give everything they have. Unfortunately that kind of attitude can make things more difficult in the dressage because what they would like to offer usually ends up a bit too much. The problem is one of containing them and persuading them to accept enough discipline to produce a consistent test.

Murphy and friends at Phoebe Stewart's farm, when he was convalescing after his pin-firing operation in 1991.

At a three-day event Ian has to give Murphy plenty of work the day before his dressage test, but he usually settles down and relaxes more easily than Glenburnie. Murphy loves performing for a crowd and when he enters the arena at a big event he grows about a hand in height. 'That's the moment you must not panic and grab at the reins,' says Ian. 'You just have to give him time to go past the judges and the people in the grandstand, and to accustom himself to the atmosphere; then you can start working him in. You can't dictate to him too soon.'

Murphy is the sort of horse that dressage judges either love or hate. He has superb paces, and the power is there for all to see, but he can give the appearance of being in two halves. 'He has a big, powerful forehand and big, powerful quarters, but he is very weak in the middle, so it is difficult to get the bits connected. Although he looks impressive I think the judges sometimes worry that it's a bit of a con job,' says Ian.

The first three times he rode Murphy at a three-day event the old FEI test was still in use, and Murphy had begun to anticipate some of the movements. He knew when he was about to do an extended canter across the arena and would come bounding out of the corner and charge off across the diagonal. Whatever Ian did, even if he sat lifelessly, he would still feel a surge of power coming through and there was nothing he could do about it. 'The first time he did it I panicked slightly and tried to hold onto him, but he never attempted to run off. He knew that he was allowed to do a big canter across the arena, and then had to slow down, so he just did it automatically, and it was better not to fight him. As long as I had my legs in position and had him on the correct bend, I just let him come through it, but he was the one who had decided to accelerate. It was nothing to do with me. The ultimate invisible aids!'

> John Reed – vet to Ian Stark
> *Murphy is reputed to be headstrong, but always behaves himself with me when being examined for any reason. Injections can be given without flinching (by either party!).*

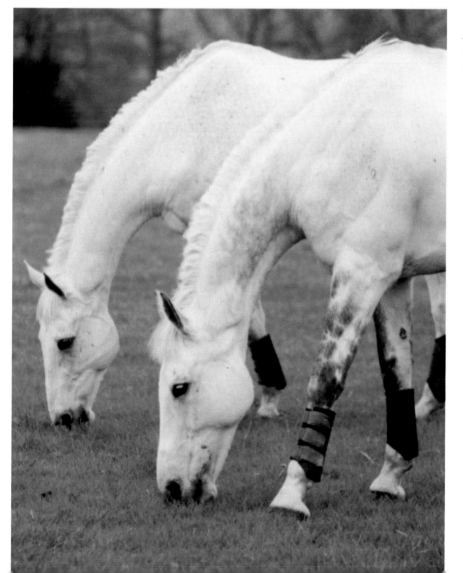

Best friends. The two greys are turned out every day during the season, and they always wear protective boots.

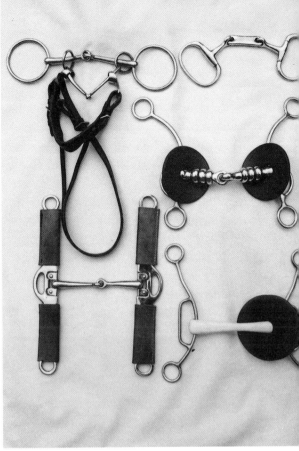

Above: *Ian usually lunges Murphy before his dressage at one-day events, but not at three-day events, when there is more time to give him the work he needs.*

Murphy's most dramatic moments in competition have, naturally, occurred on the cross-country. However, Ian has been unseated from the horse only twice – once when Murphy slipped on the flat at Boekelo, and once at Belton Park the following spring (1989) when Murphy made a mistake at the Sunken Circle and collided with the rails coming out.

There have been some other worrying incidents, though. At Ian's first Badminton with Murphy, in 1989, Murphy became excited when following the mounted steward as they were approaching the end of Phase C, the second roads and tracks. 'We came down Worcester Avenue and through the big gate into the park,' explains Ian. 'At that point you are joined by a mounted steward who goes trotting off in front of you, blowing his whistle to clear the route to the ten-minute box. When Murphy saw the steward in front of him he put in four fly-bucks until we had caught up with him. So then I had to say to the steward, "Sorry, you stay behind me and blow your whistle." Now whenever I come down there on Murphy I just shout to the steward, "Don't move until I have passed you!"

'I had a similar problem on the cross-country that year. We had jumped the Ski Jump coming from the right-hand side, and went straight from there to the Lake. As we were coming up the hill to approach the water one of the mounted stewards cantered along in front of us nearly all the way to the Lake, blowing his whistle. Some horses would have found that quite cheering and benefited from the extra incentive, but Murphy just thought, "Right, we're off." I got quite out of control following the steward's horse, so we approached the water much faster than I had intended.'

At Gatcombe Park during the final trial for the 1991 European Championships Ian came very close to parting company with Murphy for a third time. He was lying second to Mary Thomson at the start of the cross-country, so was aiming for a fast round to try to win the British Open Championship – a title that had so far eluded him. To save time he took the big Sheep Feeder, fence twelve, at an angle coming on the turn, but he slightly overdid the angle and Murphy's back feet slipped on take-off, hitting the Sheep Feeder. Although Murphy was never in danger of falling, the impact sent Ian up his neck as they landed.

'I was leaning out to the right,' Ian recalls. 'I think I must have been pulling on the rein because Murphy kept turning right and we went straight through a gap in the ropes where spectators were allowed to cross the course. I can remember, as I was hanging round his neck, seeing some people standing by the gap, and I caught a glimpse of a small child underneath me. Somehow I managed to scramble back into the saddle, and we completed a large circuit of an empty field before returning to the cross-country track. As I came back through the gap I shouted, "Is the child all right?" Someone shouted back, "Fine," so I carried on.' Precious time had been lost, however, and Ian had to settle for sixth place.

For three consecutive years, between 1989 and 1991, Ian rode both his grey horses, Murphy and Glenburnie, at Badminton. They are both demanding horses on which to compete. On the cross-country Murphy usually pulls a lot, although 1991 did see a vast improvement. Glenburnie is equally exhausting to ride across country, if not more so, because of his habit of snatching the reins out of Ian's hands. Although he will listen to Ian and allow him to influence the way he tackles a combination, Glenburnie's method of trying to dictate the pace between fences is to plunge his head down and wrench the reins from Ian's hands, a process guaranteed

Near left: *A collection of bits used by Murphy and Glenburnie. Clockwise from top left: the Citation; Dr Bristol; Cherry roller American gag (with bit guards); American gag with Nathe mouthpiece (and bit guards); an Elevator bit (used only once in competition with Glenburnie). The Citation has a nutcracker effect. The reins are attached to the large rings of the main bit, and the secondary bit is attached to the larger bit and to the noseband. When the rider pulls on the reins the secondary bit presses forward against the roof of the mouth and the noseband tightens over the nose, while the face strap puts pressure on the poll.*

to cause problems for the rider's back. That is something Ian could well do without, having taken nearly a year to recover from the serious neck injury he sustained in May 1989 in a fall from a young horse at the Charterhall event.

'I think the reason Glenburnie snatches is because he has never really learnt to take a proper contact,' says Ian. 'As a young horse he held himself behind the contact, even in a rubber snaffle, which is why his stride was short and hurried. He never worked through into the hand. Now that he has become faster and stronger across country he takes a contact but he doesn't like it, so he tries to snatch it away. I have tried stronger bits, but they usually make him worse. He will either wrench everything out of your hands or bury his head between his knees so he doesn't see the fences.'

A change to a new bit, a Waterford snaffle (a type of chain snaffle), for Badminton 1992 did, however, see a great improvement in Glenburnie's way of going. The chain seemed to prevent Glenburnie from leaning on the bit, so Ian was able to hold him without struggling to bring his head up all the time.

Facing page: *Ian and Glenburnie go through the water at Brigstock, 1992.*

Far left: *Ian's groom, Mark Holliday, applies Vetrap bandages over the top of Porter boots to protect the horse's legs on the cross-country.*

Left: *The finished bandage, taped in place; at three-day events they are stitched down the outside for additional security. Ian always uses the petal-type overreach boots, so that if the horse treads on a boot, one or two of the 'petals' will rip off rather than the whole boot. Here a good coating of hoof oil is being applied for appearances' sake. The forelegs are not usually greased for one-day events.*

Lord Patrick Beresford – chef d'équipe of the British team

Murphy has been to so many team training concentrations that I have got to know him and his histrionic mannerisms extremely well. In my mind there are four outstanding recollections that I have of him.

Number one is the first time we ever met. Ginny was hunting him with the Beaufort, and as we cantered across a field on the way to the first covert I can remember exclaiming to her: 'What power! What an action! What a horse!' Thus it came as no great surprise when, less than a year later, he stormed to victory at Burghley.

Number two is when he put Ginny into orbit at the Ski Jump fence at Badminton in 1988. Lucinda Green had suffered a similar fate earlier on, and I recall thinking rather gloomily: 'At this rate we'll have wiped out our entire Olympic team.'

Number three is a year later when Ian rode him at Badminton. He was third to go. I had worked out that, from the back of a good horse, I could see them over the Ski Jump, the Lake and the new and awesome-looking Coffin. At all three Ian lobbed him in on a lovely long rein, as if he hadn't a care in the world. It was a feat of courage and horsemanship that brought a lump to the throat, and Murphy went straight and foot-perfect through each one. In hindsight I suspect it was to Ian's advantage that in 1989 these fences were sited in the early part of the course – subsequently I have come to believe that Murphy knows exactly when he has reached half-way, and races home from there on in.

Number four, and perhaps the most enduring of all, is his cross-country round at the 1990 World Championships in Stockholm. Ian had come into the ten-minute box ashen-faced. He had already been run away with on Phase B, the steeplechase, and ahead lay a course with so many corners, bends, climbs, descents and traverses that the chances of being able to control a power-house like Murphy seemed virtually non-existent. What ensued on that hot, humid and energy-sapping afternoon was the most heart-stopping display of sheer guts on the part of both horse and rider that I have ever had to watch. I expect it took years off my life, but it won us the team and individual silver medals, and Murphy's 'bounce' at the mighty drop and road-crossing is something that no one who witnessed it will ever forget.

Of Ian's other 'grey boy', the classically handsome Glenburnie, I also have two abiding memories. The first is of him taking a straight line through the Serpentine fence at the European Championships at Burghley in 1989 – the only horse to do so in a field of fifty-four. Afterwards we were criticised from a team point of view for encouraging or even allowing Ian to take this route, but in fact it was in no sense of bravado that he decided to do so. He had seen his line on his very first course-walk and was convinced that it was easier for the long-striding Glenburnie than the alternative series of twists and turns. Their achievement was greeted with a thunderous roar from the massed ranks of spectators.

My other wonderful memory of Glen is of course his cross-country round in the European Championships at Punchestown in 1991. Again he went straight through the massive Newgrange and Parallel Rails fence, and took

> *the huge corner at the Five Lamps, one of only two horses to make such an attempt. He cruised home still pulling Ian's arms out, having assured us of another double gold.*
>
> *One thing both greys have in common is that by the time it comes to prize-giving they are so hyped-up that I invariably feel the Chef d'Équipe, on his feet in front of them, should be paid some form of danger money! But, joking apart, they have both been and are wonderful members of the British team. We are indeed lucky to have them.*

The two greys are the best of friends even when battling for honours at a competition. They nearly always travel on the box together to events, and Glenburnie is quite reluctant to leave Murphy when the time comes for him to go and compete. Coming back to the lorry is even worse. 'Glenburnie starts whinnying for Murphy as soon as he comes out of the dressage arena,' says Ian. 'It's pathetic really. I thought he would have grown out of it by now, but he seems to get worse as he gets older.' Murphy is slightly more relaxed about it all, but as a youngster he couldn't bear to be left on his own in the box at an event, and would stamp and whinny and quiver with anxiety. Someone always had to stay with him to reassure him he was not being deserted.

At competitions both horses wear protective boots whenever possible, even while working in for the dressage. 'When you have got a big competition at stake, you do try to take extra care,' says Jenny. 'The horses are so fit, they could easily shy at something and knock themselves. Glenburnie is the worst for that. We have to put his boots back on as soon as he comes out of the dressage arena, otherwise he is likely to leap about and damage himself as he has done so often in the past.'

When Ian is riding both greys at an event he has to walk the course differently for each horse. 'I have to say, well Glenburnie will jump this fence this way and put in so many strides, whereas Murphy will probably do it another way,' says Ian. 'As long as I am aware of the difference, it's all right.'

If other horses attempted to do some of the things that Murphy does they would end up in all sorts of difficulties, but Murphy can take out strides and get away with it because of his exceptional ability. 'He's a very clever horse,' says Ian. 'I think he knows what he can and cannot get away with. If he launches himself over a fence it is done with a purpose – he has weighed up the situation and he knows where he's going and how many strides he's going to take.

Equipment for the ten-minute halt box. From top left: buckets; double bridle; spare reins; bridle; breastplate and martingale attachment; martingale; breastgirth; girth; overgirth; Thermatex rug; various bits; spare set of shoes (normally ready studded); sponges; sweat scraper; Animalintex; wool bandages; spare saddle and numnah; rainsheet; kaolin; hoofpick and stud box; elasticated roller; Vetrap bandages; event paste; fly spray; canvas sheet (beneath all). Additional items (not shown) include: insulation tape; plaiting bands; scissors; needle and thread; bootlace (to tie bridle to top plait); spare overreach boots and whip; still fruit drinks and spare gloves for rider.

Ian's cross-country saddle, which has been adapted to his design by the makers Miller Crosby. It has a big, flat-ish seat and suede-covered flat knee pads so that the rider has the flexibility to adjust his position. 'If you have a deep-seated saddle it can make things more difficult, especially over a drop fence when you are likely to be hit in the back by the high cantle,' says Ian. He uses Aerborn girths, which allow the horse's skin to breathe, and always puts a surcingle over the top of the saddle for additional security. Strong, rawhide stirrup leathers are used and a fleecy numnah.

Near right: *Murphy being pampered by the family.*

Far right: *'Are there any pictures of me?'*

It's just a question of going with him. I have to be in a slightly more forward position than I would sometimes like to be just so that if he takes off too soon I won't get left behind. It took me quite a long time to get used to his enormous stride and his power. He feels twenty hands high when you are on top and the fences come at you very quickly, so you are taking off faster and sooner than you had anticipated.

'I know it sometimes looks as if I take risks with him, but it doesn't feel that way to me. I couldn't jump a fence without seeing my stride and knowing exactly where I was going to take off. For a straightforward, galloping fence, I can usually assess where we will take off about ten strides away, and for a more technical fence perhaps five or six strides away. The most important thing with Murphy is to make sure I have anchored him enough to bring him into an obstacle in the right gear and in balance, so that even though I give him his head when we get to the fence I have already seen my stride. He is unlikely to do anything out of the ordinary on his approach; it is once he gets into a combination that he might take out a stride, but I can usually tell if that is likely to happen by the way he has jumped in. What I would never do is come into a combination with a 'yahoo' attitude, because then we'd be all over the place.'

> Jane Holderness-Roddam – Chairman of the Selectors' Committee
> *There have been many very good eventers, but to me, Ian and Murphy have have done as much for eventing as my sister, Jennie [Loriston-Clarke], and Dutch Courage did for dressage. Murphy must rank as an equal to those other great horses, Milton and Desert Orchid – we owe them all a debt of gratitude for the memories they have given us.*

Although Murphy has a huge stride he is exceptionally athletic and can put in the shortest of strides when he wants to – partly because of his own natural ability, and also because of the training he received with Ginny, who spent months teaching him to shorten. 'Murphy is so light on his feet and so quick; he's like a cat,' says Ian. 'Sometimes when he puts in a quick stride you are hardly aware that he's touched down. He's very nimble. I think that's why he finds it all so easy.

'He also has the power to get himself out of awkward situations. The trouble is, if he found himself in serious difficulties, perhaps because I'd let him approach an obstacle too fast, he would probably jump me off. He doesn't want to hit a fence or fall. If he got in much too close to a fence he would just go straight up and do such a huge jump that the power of it would shoot me out of the saddle. I think the only reason that hasn't happened to me yet is that I don't hold on to the front end. If I did, I'm sure he would have pulled me out of the plate quite frequently because he uses his head and neck so much.

'It took me quite a long time to work out the best way to ride Murphy across country, and I eventually decided that the right thing to do was to let him have his head and take all the decisions once we reached an obstacle. To start with it was a very frightening thing to do and it went against all my natural instincts, but now that I know him better I trust him completely, and I think he trusts me to let him do his own thing. I realise that it can sometimes look like a dangerous policy, but I honestly think that if I tried to hang on to him I wouldn't survive.'

It is a policy that has paid dividends, even if it has not always met with universal approval. Leaving the decisions to Murphy can make life unpredictable at times, but it is that unpredictability, combined with his exceptional ability and power, that makes Murphy such an exciting horse to watch.

Olympic Finale

At the beginning of 1992 it was generally assumed that Ian would be going to the Olympics – the question was: which horse would he ride? Murphy was slightly more reliable across country, but he had been very tired after his round in Stockholm; whereas Glenburnie, being Thoroughbred, had still been full of running when he finished the course at Punchestown. Barcelona would be hot and humid, with a tough, four-and-a-half-mile course that would sap the energy of even the fittest horses, but surely Murphy was too good to leave out of the team?

Preparations for the Games went well for both horses, apart from a nasty fall at the Ha-Ha at Badminton for Glenburnie, who fortunately was none the worse for the experience. Both horses had been excused from running at Badminton, since neither had anything to prove to the selectors, but Ian had opted to take Glenburnie while leaving Murphy at home – much to the latter's disgust.

After a good outing at the final trial at Savernake, where Murphy won his section, Ian was in the happy position of being the only team member to have two horses going to Barcelona – the decision as to which he would ride would be made once they were there. Despite the last-minute withdrawal of Ginny Leng from the team because of an injury to Master Craftsman, Britain still had a strong squad in Mary Thomson (with King William), Richard Walker (with Jacana), Karen Dixon (with Get Smart) and Ian with his two greys, and the team went to Barcelona as favourites to win the gold medal.

Once Ian had seen the cross-country course at the El Montanya golf club, where the three-day event was held, he decided that it would suit Murphy better than Glenburnie. It was a big course, one of the biggest seen in recent Olympics, and many of the combinations had been designed to favour a long-striding horse. The only drawback for Murphy would be the tight turns and twisty track.

As the last to go for the British team Murphy helped to take Britain into the lead at the end of the two days of dressage by producing the best test he has ever done at a three-day event. 'I hadn't ridden him in for long because it was so hot,' said Ian, 'but luckily,

At fence 16 on the way down to the first lake crossing, where Ian took the fast route.
(Photo: Barn Owl)

when we went into the arena he stayed relaxed. The heat probably helped to keep him calm.' Individually they were in second place.

The following day it was Murphy's job once again to salvage British hopes, just as he had done in Stockholm. Richard Walker, first to go for the team, had come to grief at the second water complex, fence 16, when Jacana stopped at the substantial rail at the brink of the slope going down to the water and Richard flew over the fence without him. The mistake cost him and the British team dearly, as he finished the cross-country on a score of 208.8. Consequently, both Karen and Mary were under instructions to go slowly and carefully for a clear round, tactics that got them both home safely but with significant time penalties.

By then New Zealand already had three riders home with fast clear rounds, so it was essential for Ian and Murphy to go clear to keep Britain in with a chance of a medal. Spectators were not to be disappointed. Murphy was himself to the last, bounding over the obstacles with his usual mixture of enthusiasm, agility and sheer power. 'He was pulling my arms out,' Ian admitted afterwards. The only serous crisis came at the 18th, a bank and rails coming out of the water, where Murphy nearly took the fence out by the roots after a muddle-up with his striding. From the force of the blow a fall looked inevitable, but somehow Murphy kept on his feet – and, somehow, Ian managed to stay in the saddle.

By the end of the course the heat and terrain had taken their toll of the ebullient grey, and his pace slackened off noticeably over the last few fences. Ian did not press him, just letting him go at his own speed, and they finished the course with 36.4 time faults. However, considering that no one achieved the optimum time, Murphy's penalty score was not excessive, and it brought Britain into the silver medal position and Ian into fifth place after the speed and endurance. 'I lost a lot of time trying to hold Murphy and pull him up for his fences,' said Ian. 'I had hoped he had become older and wiser, but as soon as he came out of the start box on the steeplechase I knew he was his old self.'

Even before disaster struck for Murphy the following morning, Ian had decided to retire him. 'That's the last time I'll ride him across country,' he told Michael Calvin of the *Daily Telegraph*. 'He doesn't owe me anything. There's not a human being who can match up to him. It's a sad old day, isn't it?'

Somewhat prophetically, Michael Calvin ended his article with the following paragraph: 'It was, indeed, rather like an Irish

Coming out of the lake (fence 18). Murphy jumped onto the bank on a long stride and then put in a quick half stride before the second element, which he hit very hard. It was his only serious mistake on the course. (Photo: Barn Owl)

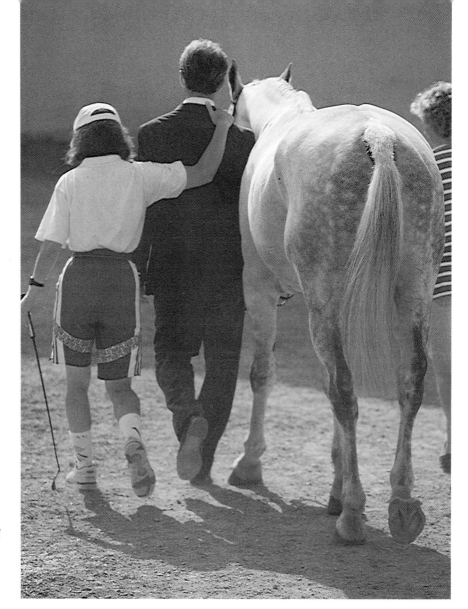

'A sad old day'. Ian is comforted by team physio, Jo Farrington, as he and Jenny lead Murphy away from the final horse inspection. Murphy was spun by the ground jury because of a strained fetlock, and as a result Britain's hopes of a team medal went by the board. (Photo: Barn Owl)

funeral, a celebration of a life lived well. Let us hope today doesn't bring the hangovers associated with such occasions.'

Alas, his worst fears were confirmed: Murphy failed the horse inspection the following morning. The problem – a suspected strain to his off-fore fetlock. So Murphy went out of the competition, and with him went Britain's hopes of an Olympic medal. It certainly was a sad old day, but at least Murphy had maintained his record of going clear across country at every major three-day event he had ever done with Ian. His nine-year career may not have ended gloriously with an Olympic medal, but he will always be remembered as the horse who has given the sport some of its most exciting moments.

LOCAL COLLECTION